A Living History of Our World

The Story of the Ancients
Creation through Rome

by Angela O'Dell

illustrations by Angela, Savannah, and Kylah O'Dell,
and Melissa Carlson

© Jelly Bean Jar PUBLICATIONS™ 2015

A Living History of Our World
The Story of the Ancients

Written by Angela O'Dell
Illustrated by Angela, Savannah, and Kylah O'Dell,
and Melissa Carlson

Dedicated to Dave,
my hero, best friend, and # 1 cheerleader.
I love you.

Soli Deo Gloria

Table of Contents

Table of Contents

Table of Contents

Table of Contents

Table of Contents

Many thanks to Kyrsten Carlson and Renee O'Dell

for their superior editing skills and their willingness

to help with this book.

You both are such a blessing!

Introduction

Welcome to <u>A Living History of Our World</u>. Although this is not the first volume in this series, it is the first volume dedicated to world history. I hope you enjoy your journey with me through the beginning part of our incredible history here on this earth.

If you and your family have completed any or all of the volumes in this series, you are already comfortable with the layout and the style of the books. However, for the convenience of all newcomers, I will explain how this course is to be used. The American history volumes in this series were created with a certain age range in mind, but this volume and the other volumes covering world history are written to be used with all ages together.

The history of the world should be learned by all people. As parents, it is our responsibility to our children to make sure that they understand history did not start with Christopher Columbus sailing the ocean blue in 1492. History is much older than that! The time period covered in this volume is the time my children like to call "Bible Times," and, indeed, the Bible was my main source of information in the writing of this volume.

You will see that most chapters have this symbol after the reading, followed by a Scripture to be read and discussed together. These Scripture references will supply Biblical backing for the story in this book. Please take the time for these important readings.

"A Living God for Living Education"

Charlotte Mason once said, "<u>The indwelling of Christ is a thought particularly fit for the children, because their large faith does not stumble at the mystery, their imagination leaps readily to the marvel, that the King Himself should inhabit a little child's heart.</u>" God is alive. Not only is He alive now, but He has always been so.

Introduction

Studying world history, through the worldview glasses of Biblical accounts, allows a child to see history for what it truly is - HIStory.

My goal in writing this curriculum is to make an easy-to-use, comprehensive history resource for you to use with your whole family at one time, with little to no preparation and no necessary supplement beyond your Bible. (If you are doing this study as a family, you may even choose to have a journal for each of the parents involved in the study.)

How to use "A Living History of Our World: Story of the Ancients"

This curriculum has two parts: this history storybook and the Student's Journal. There are twenty-eight chapters and four built-in reviews, making it quite attainable to finish in one school year. The journal pages are an assortment of areas to write/ journal, hands-on projects and pictures to color. There is also a section of timeline projects (instructions included), written narration prompts, and several optional projects.

Unique to the world history volumes in this series, are the reproducible* "Student Research" packets included in the back of each Student Journal. There are two packets; one is appropriate for your junior high student, and the other is deep enough for your senior high schooler. Elementary students may simply use the Student Journal pages to record what they are learning, while their older siblings will also use these convenient research forms to dig even deeper into their studies. I have included a list of research tools for these older students that will make their studies more meaningful. In the appendix of this volume, I have included a list of additional research topics for your junior high and high school students. These additional research topics are plentiful and are meant to be assigned by you, the parent/teacher. I would suggest planning on having your junior high student

Introduction

complete one research topic per two weeks, and your senior high student complete three each month. (You make the ultimate decision, though, as you know your children's abilities.)

Your younger children will find everything they need to complete their journal pages in their Bible, in an encyclopedia, or online.** By having your children use an encyclopedia a couple times a week, you can easily teach important research skills. Of course, if your children are very small, don't feel like you need to have them do this. Make this curriculum fit your family. For your convenience, I have included a schedule to work through this course. You will find the suggested schedule in the appendix of this book.

Including geography in your study

Many of the lessons have geographical locations in them. Have your globe or world map handy, so that you and your children can find them after you finish reading. You may also want to include simple map reading skills. Just say, "What continent is ____ on?" or "What hemisphere is ____ in?" By simply including this information into your conversation, you familiarize your children with geographical terms.

More on supplementing

Please remember if your younger children do only what is included in this book and in the Student's Journal, you will have done enough! However, I am aware that there are children who love to read and want to know more about a particular historical topic. For these children and for the families who enjoy historical read-alouds, I have included a list of books in the appendix of this book. These are books I have personally read to or with my children. They are arranged by subject and clearly marked for the appropriate age group. Many of them can be found in public

Introduction

libraries. Also included is a literature list for the older student. This list is also arranged according to subject or time period.

An Important Note on Narration

A Living History of Our World is written in the Charlotte Mason style. Narration is a key element of this curriculum. Please take the time to employ oral narration whenever the book suggests it. Included in the Student's Journal is a section of written narration prompts for the older child.

What preparations do you need to get ready for a wonderful year of history?

1. Have this book for you, as a teacher, and a Student's Journal for each of your children. Junior high and high school students may wish to have their own copy of this book also.

2. Determine how many research topics you want your older students to complete and make the appropriate number of copies of the "Student Research Aids" packet.

3. You will need the following items to complete your Student's Journal:

   ☐ Scissors

   ☐ Glue

   ☐ Colored pencils, markers and crayons

   ☐ Hole punch

   ☐ Stapler

   ☐ Hole re-enforcers

   ☐ Construction paper

   ☐ Poster board (optional)

Introduction

- ☐ Contact paper

- ☐ Brass fasteners

- ☐ Encyclopedias (books or CD ROM)

- ☐ Old magazines for pictures

- ☐ World map or globe

- ☐ Bible

- ☐ Two, 3-ring notebook for each of your jr. and sr. high students

- ☐ One, 3-ring notebook for your elementary students

- ☐ NOTE: 1.5 or 2 inch notebooks with clear plastic sleeve covers work best.

*The supplied research aid packet is reproducible only for the student using the Student Journal. Please do not reproduce for siblings.

**Please use close parent supervision when young children are using the internet.

Note: some chapters will be heavier in Bible reading assignments than others.

An additional, highly suggested resource, which would be extremely helpful with child-friendly Bible readings, is the Egermeirer's Bible Story Book. This wonderful Bible Story book was first published in 1922, and is illustrated with beautiful classic art.

Introduction

"We see, then, that the children's lessons should provide material for their mental growth, should exercise the several powers of their minds, should furnish them with fruitful ideas, and should afford them knowledge, really valuable for its own sake, accurate, and interesting, of the kind that the child may recall as a man with profit and pleasure." Charlotte Mason

(The Original Homeschooling Series, Volume 1, Part V Lessons as Instruments of Education, p.177)

❖ All quotes are categorized in the "Works Cited" page in the appendix.

❖ All illustrations and pictures are private property.

Preface

This is a story of the Ancients. However, it is not a dry, dusty, "comprehensive" view of the history of the world during the time which we call "Ancient." Instead, this book is meant to set a backdrop of sorts in the child's (and parent's) mind of what the general happenings of that time period were.

Why does anyone NEED to know about this time period? The answer to that question is both simple and difficult to answer. It is simple because it happened, and if it happened, it is part of who we all are, whether or not we know it. It is difficult, because sometimes we do not see a need to learn anything that we do not see as directly influencing or affecting us. What we need to realize is that we are not islands unto ourselves; we are this generation of God's family. We need to know the past, the habits, the drive of the human race. God did not create us to be born, live, and die without leaving this world a truly better place. To leave it a better place, we need to know the One Who can make it better. This is truly the only way to make a difference.

We all need to know WHY everyone needs forgiveness. We all need to know the Hope of all the nations. Only God can save the soul of those who make up the human race. I like to say that if we do not learn history, it is impossible to learn from history. If we do not learn from history, we cannot change the future.

There is no way to include all of the happenings of this time period for several reasons. The biggest reason is that only God knows everything that ever happened, every person who ever lived and every civilization that ever rose and fell. Only He knows the details and what truly happened. All we can do is study what has been recorded, and many of these recorded facts are tainted by opinion, ungodly worldview glasses, and human error. The only 100% true account of these times that we have is the Bible.

The Bible is Holy Spirit breathed and is completely true and the ultimate guide to "Ancient History." This is why I have chosen to use the Bible as my absolute baseline of truth, not just for this book, but for all of my writing, and indeed, my life. In this world of relativism, I know that I desperately need something that I can trust at all times. That is why I stand on the promises of God, written to me in the holy Word of God. Whenever I have a question about something, I go to the Bible. The answer is always there. Always. No exception. It is living and breathing and completely pertinent to every issue with which mankind has ever dealt.

Another reason there is no way to include all of the happenings of this time period is obvious; the book would be a million pages long and as boring and dry as powder. This is not the goal I have for you as my readers.

So what is my goal? My ultimate goal in this and every book that I have written or ever will write is to lead you straight to the very heart of our Father. Since He is the only One Who knows the past, the present, and the future, I believe that He is the only One Who can truly teach us. I want you to see His hand on mankind. I want you feel His heart break as He watches the people, whom He created for His delight and pleasure, turn their backs on Him and choose sin. I want you to marvel as His plan for a Redeemer begins to be revealed in history. I want you to be amazed at the very-human people He decides to use to do amazing things in the story of the world... just because He can! I want you to hear His heartbeat as He chooses a young, unmarried girl to be the earthly mother of His own Son. I want you to feel the pain as the crown of thorns rips into the skin of God in human flesh: Jesus. I want you to look into the eyes of my Savior and my Friend as He breathes His last, and like me, I want you to KNOW that He did it for you, too. I want all of us to hear His voice rending the heavens with His cry, "Forgive them, Father, for they know not what they do!"

Preface

Through the study of history, we, as co-inhabitants of this earth, need to understand, that man, left to his own devices, will always choose the wrong path. Time after time, the stories tell us one thing: we need a savior. We cannot live in a life with no worship. We will either worship Him, or we will worship something else. I know that this is not a Bible study book, but I do believe this could not be more pertinent to any other subject but HIStory. As we study the history of "Bible times," we will see the fingerprints and the footprints of the Creator of it all. Please promise me that you will recognize and diligently guard against the tendency to read the familiar stories of the Bible with complacency and familiarity. It is so important to let the Word of God fall afresh on our hearts every time we read it. The Word is living! Through His Word, we can know Him.

This is the reason for this study of the Ancients, to know the Ancient of Days.

Choosing your level of study...

This volume, and the three following it, are written to be used by a wide age range. They are meant to be flexible to your needs. Following is an outline of the different levels of study based on the skill/age level of your children.

If you are studying together as a family, including lower elementary, middle elementary, jr. high, and high school children, follow this plan:

- Read the chapter portion and any assigned Bible reading out loud.

- Assign each child work according to their level (outlined on the next page).

- Review together as you construct your timeline project.

Level 1 - early elementary

- Listen to the story

- Narrate orally

- Work on Journal pages (draw, write or have parent be the scribe) and construct timeline
- (Optional) Do hands-on project

<u>Level 2 - mid to upper elementary</u>

- Listen to the story
- Narrate orally
- Work on Journal pages (draw, write, research) and construct timeline.
- Do written narration prompts
- (Optional) Do hands-on project (ideas included)

<u>Level 3 - Jr. high</u>

- Listen to the story
- Work on Journal pages (draw, write, research) and construct timeline.
- Do written narration prompts (optional)
- Use Jr. High level research "packet" to dig deeper into chosen topics
(Research packet and topics are provided)
- (Optional) Read assigned literature
- (Optional) Do hands-on project (ideas included)

<u>Level 4 - High School</u>

- Listen to the story (or read to yourself if you are working independently)
- Work on Journal pages (draw, write, research) and construct timeline.
- Do written narration prompts (optional)
- Use High School level research "packet" to dig deeper into chosen topics
(Research packet and topics are provided)
- (Optional) Read assigned literature
- (Optional) Do hands-on project (ideas included)

In the Beginning...

Have you ever seen pictures, taken from outer space, of our home, planet Earth? Neil Armstrong, the American astronaut famous for first stepping out on the moon, commented as he gazed at Earth from the window of the space ship, "It suddenly struck me that that tiny pea, pretty and blue, was the Earth. I put up my thumb and shut one eye, and my thumb blotted out the planet Earth. I didn't feel like a giant. I felt very, very small."

Can you imagine what the earth was like before God chose to form our planet so He could create life here? It says in the Bible that "the earth was without form." Any study of world history could not start anywhere but with this verse from the Holy Bible. The moment God spoke the earth into being, was the very moment when history started. We must never forget, though, that this is not when God "started," for He is the "Beginning and the End." The very first words in the Bible are "In the beginning, God..." This is the beginning of everything - God. He was. He is. He will always be.

Non-believers have, for years, tried to explain away the amazing event that we, as Christians, hold as truth - Creation! When God put His creation plan into action, He did not need anyone's help; He simply spoke, and it happened. In only six days, He formed the earth, separated the land and sea, set the weather into motion, filled the seas and oceans with amazing and wonderful water creatures, designed the intricate feathers of the birds and showed them how to fly, ran the

roots of the trees and plants deep into the soil, and placed all of the land creatures into their natural habitats. Yet He wasn't finished! He had used all of these other aspects of His creativeness to make this glorious home for His final and most important creation - man.

The Bible says God formed man out of the dust of the earth and made him in His likeness. Then God breathed into the man to give him life and named him Adam. The Bible does not tell us that any of the other creatures were breathed into, and none of them were made in the likeness of God Himself. Man was a special creation, indeed! Later, God created a woman by taking one of the man's ribs and creating a helper for the man. Adam named her Eve.

It was God's plan that they live in and take care of the beautiful creation He had made for them. He loved them and took care of them, providing everything they needed for life. Thus, nestled between two beautiful, crystal-clear rivers, He placed their perfect home, the lush and fruitful Garden of Eden. This special place was the personal paradise for these first two people who God created, and in a way, this garden was the first civilization on the earth.

Not everything in the garden was good for the man and woman to eat, though. God warned them to not eat of a certain tree in the middle. He told them if they ate of the fruit, they would surely die. It was not that the fruit on this particular tree was poisonous; however, it was the disobedience to God which would slowly poison them, separating them from the holiness of God. We know the story of how the serpent, who was really the devil, came and tempted the woman to eat of the forbidden fruit. Her disobedience to God was the beginning of the slow decay of God's perfect world, but God still loved these two special people for whom He had held such high hopes. He had already decided on a plan for human redemption.

After they had disobeyed God, Adam and Eve were driven from the garden. They no longer had everything supplied by the hand of God Himself. They now had to work and sweat for their food. They felt pain and knew of their nakedness. Sin had already spread into the world, which God had designed. He must have been so sad to see that these two people, whom He had created to take care of the earth, now had to till and sweat to live, but God still took care of them. He blessed them with a family, two sons whom they named Cain and Abel.

Biblical knowledge note:

We can thank Moses for recording the Creation story for us. Even though Moses lived thousands of years later, he was the man who God instructed to write down every word as He recounted the creation of the world. Remember, all of Scripture is God breathed. This means that the Holy Spirit guided him to know the words to write.

Genesis 1: 1 - 31 (Creation account)

Luke 24: 27, John 5: 46 (Verification of the writer of Genesis)

Chapter 1

Narration Break: discuss how God created the world. What are some theories that man has invented to explain away the creation of the world?

As we study what we call "ancient" history, we will be using the most reliable history "text book" that has ever been written: the very Word of God. There will be times this study is easy to understand, and there will also be times when it requires us to put on our thinking caps. We will learn about the civilizations which grew in the world. We will watch the perfect and beautiful world, which God so lovingly created, change.

When sin entered the world through the disobedience of Adam and Eve, every child born afterward was born with the sinful nature, which was the result of that original sin. Adam and Eve's sons were born outside of the garden. They were very different from each other, and the older brother, Cain, was given to anger and rebellion. The account of what happened with these two brothers is recorded in Genesis 4. Cain murdered Abel. When God confronted Cain about what he had done, He told Cain he would be sent out into the earth with a mark placed upon him by the Lord Himself.

Genesis 4 (The account of how Adam and Eve's family grew and multiplied)

During these years, as Adam and Eve's family spread out over the known earth, sin multiplied. The Garden of Eden, which had been an oasis of safety and prosperity, marked by a closeness to the Creator, was a faint memory. Life outside of the garden was difficult. The people had to farm the land, raise animals, and take what they needed from the earth. They lived in caves or huts made of rocks and animal skin. They ate whatever they could find to keep alive.

From Biblical accounts, the location of the Garden of Eden is thought to have been between the Tigris and Euphrates Rivers, in an area known as the Fertile Crescent. As more and more people inhabited the earth, they spread out to cover more of the land. Of course, no one knew how big the earth really is, and the population was clustered in what is now called the Middle East. Look at the map below, and compare it to a current map of the same area. What countries are located there now?

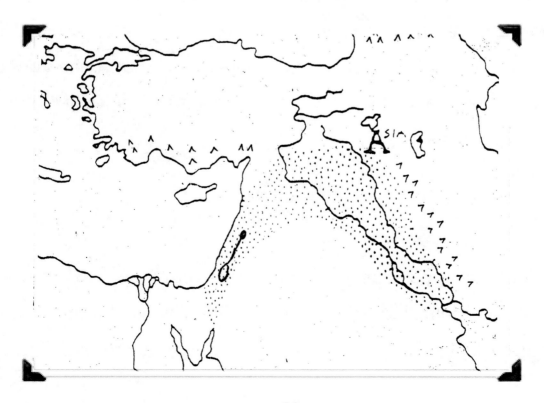

Some people call this time period the "Stone Age." In a way, this truly was a "stone" age, because stone was used in a multitude of ways. The metals of the earth had not been fully discovered, and because of this, stone was used for weapons and tools.

Biblical historians believe Cain's descendants were the first civilization to discover and use metals which could be used for tools and weapons. This civilization was also known to have music and other forms of entertainments. However, they were not good people. They were not godly, and their sins rose like a stench to God.

As the human population multiplied and spread out over the earth, sin grew with it. Fifteen hundred years had passed since the birth of Seth, Adam and Eve's third son. It says in Genesis 6 evil was everywhere, and God could find only one man who pleased Him. God is merciful and kind by nature, He is a just God. The sin of the earth made Him so angry, He was sorry He had created man at all. God is also a God of second chances, and so He chose the man who pleased Him to be the one He saved from destruction. In our next chapter, we will learn about this new beginning for the earth, which God had so lovingly created.

Genesis 5 (The account of men between Adam and Noah)

Narration Break: take the time to read and discuss what the Bible says about these first people groups of the earth. Read through "Apologetics through Archaeology" #1.

Starting Over

In this chapter, we are going to learn about one of the most amazing happenings in all of history - the Great Flood. Even though most people groups on the earth have a similar "tale" in their histories, we know the true story of this happening is in Genesis. These people groups' legends and tales are somewhat similar to the account in Genesis, but none of them are completely accurate.

The Bible does not say much about the peoples of the world before God sent the flood. From Genesis chapter five through the beginning of chapter six, we can conclude that the godly people intermarried with the ungodly to the point there was no difference between the two groups.

Something we find astounding is the length of time people lived in the days before the flood. Reading through Genesis chapter five, we find each man lived hundreds of years! Sin was on the earth, but it had not had thousands of years to cause its mutations and diseases that it has today. In those days, there were far fewer handicaps of all kinds, and because people lived longer, they were able to have many more children.

The Bible records that there was evil everywhere. Wickedness was in almost every heart. God found only one man who honored Him in his heart and his life. This man was Noah. The Bible says, in Genesis 6:9, he was "upright" and "he walked with God." God warned Noah that He was going to destroy the earth with a flood. He was so tired of the self-centered, humanistic people living on the earth, He was going to wipe them all away.

God planned to do something merciful, though. He would save some of each type of animal to start over with, after the flood. Noah and his family would become the humans that would start the human race over again. God told Noah His plans and asked him to obey Him. He gave Noah specific directions to build a safe place for the chosen animals and his own family. Noah was to build an ark, a huge craft that would be big enough to hold the animals which God would send, along with Noah's family.

The dimensions of the ark were staggeringly enormous. The original Hebrew word for our word "ark" literally means "box." God had instructed Noah to build a box so big that they could have stacked five hundred twenty-two standard-sized railroad cars inside of it. The ark, which was four hundred fifty feet long, was one hundred fifty feet longer than a football field! It was also forty-five feet tall (which is as tall as a four story building) and seventy-five feet wide. Can you imagine being told to build such a huge structure?

Even though the Bible does not make it perfectly clear how long it took to build the ark, Bible scholars have determined it was probably anywhere between fifty-five and seventy-five years [1]. At any rate, Noah was six hundred years old when God instructed him to take his family into the ark.

I think it would be safe to say, as Noah and his sons built the ark, they tried to talk to their neighbors and relatives about what was going to happen. Of course, the wicked people would not listen to them and laughed at the thought of a flood. Have you ever wondered what all the people thought when they saw all of the animals coming? I would think they would have second thoughts about Noah's questioned sanity!

The animals, which God had gathered to place on the ark, were ready to load onto the craft. This was a far cry from what most modern Bible storybooks depict. Many of these books contain drawings of a few, smiling animals walking in pairs up the gangplank into a cute, little boat. In reality, there were hundreds of creatures, including mammals like huge lions, camels, giraffes, and monkeys, as well as dinosaurs, reptiles, and lizards, along with hundreds of creepy-crawly insects in many different varieties. There were so many birds and creatures of the air, it most likely took days to get them all onboard. From where did they all come, and who brought them? God Himself had gathered and brought them to this place of safety. Noah did not have to go get them and lead them to the ark. When they were all onboard, God closed the giant door.

Genesis 6 (God chooses Noah to build the ark)

Narration Break: discuss the story so far. After reading the above Bible reading, try to find an area big enough to (roughly) measure out the dimensions of the ark.

The big day had finally arrived. The animals were all onboard, along with Noah and his wife, three sons and their wives. They had obeyed God and gathered the amount of food that He had given in His directions. Noah trusted that God would do as He said; He would send the waters to cover the earth. Suddenly it started to rain, first as a sprinkle, and then as a torrent. Little rivulets ran through the dust around the ark's construction site. These swelled into bigger streams, which, in turn, became rushing rivers of dirty water, churning with topsoil and broken tree branches.

The people, who had mocked Noah's construction of the ark, now hammered on the side of the ship, but God had closed the heavy door with His own hands. He alone could open it, and He had chosen not to. Finally, the banging stopped, and Noah and his family became aware of the water sounds rushing by them on the outside of the ark. They knew their neighbors were gone. They also knew God had done exactly what He said He would do. The eight people inside the ark knelt in thanksgiving for the mercy of their God. It was approximately two thousand years after God had created the earth, that He wiped mankind and every living thing, except that which was in the ark, from the face of the earth.

The Bible says the water came down from heaven and up from the deep of the earth. Genesis 7:11 says the "fountains of the great deep broke open, and the windows of heaven were opened." Imagine with me the terror of those wicked people as earthquakes shook the ground on which they stood. The water from the great deep erupted so forcefully that it sent walls of water straight up into the air. This most likely sent such violent vibrations that volcanoes, which had lain dormant, erupted with magnificent force, raining down fire balls and lava on everything surrounding them. The earth's crust was literally ripping apart, possibly

setting entire continents and islands into motion, and the water rose.
Higher and higher, the mighty hand of God sent the water over the
tallest trees, over the mountains, until, just as He had promised, it
covered the whole earth.

Inside the ark, the animals and people probably had a horribly
bumpy ride! God must have supernaturally calmed the animals so they
would not stampede in terror. The noise would have been deafening.

With the rain and storms booming outside, and the water rushing and gushing from deep in the earth, it was certainly the hand of God that steadied the ark, steering it clear of debris that would most assuredly have smashed into the sides, completely destroying it and its occupants.

For days and days, Noah and his family and all of the animals were tossed and turned on the water. The Bible says the rain came down for forty days and nights, and the water kept rising one hundred ten days after that. There is no way we can even imagine this type of situation, because we have nothing to which we can compare it, but consider everything that we know...

Noah and his family knew they were the only human life left on the planet because God had told them He was going to destroy everyone except them. The ark was filled with literally thousands of animals, and the entire earth was covered with water. The ark only had a few windows for such a huge craft, and therefore, was dark inside. It rained and stormed for over a month. The water from inside the earth came up, creating such turbulent currents, that the ark was being tossed around like a toy boat.

Truly, the only hope that kept these eight people from pure panic was the fact that God had done everything that He had promised, and He had promised that they would be the beginning of the new human race after the flood. They had to believe what God had said. They did not have any other choice. Isn't it wonderful to know this is the same God we serve? He always keeps His promises. Even when things of the earth change, He does not. He is the same.

Finally the water stopped its incessant rising and swirling, and the ark floated more calmly on top of the flood. Over entire mountain ranges and deep valleys, the ark was still guided by the hand of God. Life onboard the ark probably settled into a routine, with Noah and his family caring for the animals. I am quite sure their routine included a time of worship and thanks to God for saving them. Day by day they could see the water going down, and then one day, the ark came to rest on a mountain. Noah knew that their time to go out onto dry land was coming closer.

One day, Noah sent out a raven to see if it would find a place to roost and not need to return to the ark. The raven did not return; it

---

Time spent on the Ark based on the account in Genesis 6-9
The rain fell from the sky for 40 days
The water rose an additional 110 days
The water receded over the the following 74 days (based on a 30 day month)
Noah sent a raven out of the Ark after 40 days
He sent out a dove 7 days later
He sent out the dove for the second time 7 days later
He sent out the dove for the third time 7 days later
29 days passed
57 days passed from when Noah took off the covering of the ark to the final day
Total number of days on the ark: 371

must have found a place to rest. A week later, Noah sent out a dove, which returned in a short time. In still another week, Noah sent out the dove again. This time the dove returned with an olive leaf in its mouth. This was a very good sign, indeed! The olive leaf meant there was vegetation, and they would soon be leaving the ark. When Noah sent the dove out yet again, the bird did not return; it too had found a resting place and no longer needed the ark.

Genesis 8:13 says "Noah removed the covering of the ark," which probably means that he chopped a hole in the side of the ark to remove the outer covering of wood and pitch. After deciding the ground was dry enough to disembark, Noah and his family stepped out on dry land for the first time in over a year. Grateful for God's protection and blessing, Noah built an altar and burned an offering of thanksgiving.

God looked with pleasure on this family kneeling around the altar. He saw their hearts of thankfulness, and He made a promise to Noah and his family that He would never again send a flood to destroy the entire earth. He placed a beautiful, brilliant rainbow in the sky as a sign of this covenant. God then instructed Noah and his sons to multiply and fill the earth again.

 Read Genesis 7 – 8 (the complete account of the flood)

Narration Break: retell the story of the flood. Read "Apologetics through Archaeology" #2.

A Tower to Heaven

After God had washed the world clean of the evil He hated so much, the earth was a very different place. The climate had changed and there was contention between humans and animals. Many creatures, which depended on vegetation to live and thrive, died off for lack of food or became smaller and weaker because of their changed diet.

Noah and his family did what God had said to do, and they multiplied and spread out over the earth. Their sons had children who had children, and soon there were many, many people on earth once again. A couple hundred years had passed since the flood, and the earth was once again inhabited by evil people. Please take the time now to read the following Scriptures. They give an accurate account of the generations of Noah's post-flood family.

Read Genesis 10 (the account of the generations of Noah's family after the flood)

As you can see, Noah's family spread far and wide. These people did not take advantage of the second chance God was giving the human race. God would have gladly taught them to live for Him and how to build a culture based on godly concepts, but many of them were not interested. Instead, they turned their backs more and more on what was godly.

As the post-flood population grew, they migrated southeastward from Mount Ararat, where the ark had come to rest after the flood. (Mount Ararat is on the eastern border of modern day Turkey.) As they moved in this southeasterly direction, they moved into the Plain of Shinar, which we also know by the name of Sumer. It was in this land that Nimrod, a descendent of Noah's son, Ham, became a mighty ruler. Nimrod was not a godly man, and he had power and ambition. It was under Nimrod's leadership that the city of Babel was built.

The citizens of Babel wanted to build a tower to reach to the sky. At this time in history, the "towers" were usually ziggurats, which were "stair-step" in design. We are not positive if the Tower of Babel was such a structure, but there is a good chance it was a ziggurat or something similar. Under Nimrod's leadership, the people were, what we call today, humanists. They thought they could elevate themselves to the level of God if they could build their tower tall enough. They did not want to be "scattered abroad upon the face of the whole earth" (Genesis 11:4). This went against what God had commanded when He said to replenish the earth.

God did not like disobedience then any more than He does now. He looked down on these people, running around, building their tower "to reach the heavens" and decided to mix them up a little. During this time, all people spoke the same language and could communicate with each other without any difficulties. God decided it was about time to diversify the language situation.

Can you just see it? Work-men were busy on the tower construction, congratulating themselves on how smart they were, when all of a sudden, the bricklayer could not understand the mortar layer, the overseer could not understand the messenger boy, and the architect

could not give directions that anyone could understand. They looked at each other in complete confusion! They probably spent the entire day yelling at each other and gesturing frantically trying to get themselves understood.

As time passed and the language issue remained, Nimrod's rule began to crumble. Everyday, life became too much of a struggle to hold the civilization together. The Bible is not clear on how

God confused the languages. We do not know if each family spoke a different dialect or if it was literally that each individual person had his own personal language now. At any rate, the language barrier caused much of the population to leave the Plain of Shinar (Sumer).To this day, the word "babel" means confusion.

Read Genesis 11: 1- 9 (the account of the Tower of Babel)
Narration Break: discuss the story so far.

God had successfully ended construction on the blasphemous tower. He watched as the people split up into groups in which they understood each other. These groups moved away in different directions and settled in other places. These would be the start of the first civilizations in other parts of the world. People groups migrated to Asia, which would become become ancient China, to the Indus Valley, which would someday become India, to Africa, where a powerful civilization would grow along the Nile River, and even to the Americas. These civilizations would become powerful nations.

Let's take a look a two of these civilizations. The first one is actually a group of city-states that had residence in the Fertile Crescent, or as we call it Mesopotamia. This is the same location of the town and tower of Babel. It is between the Tigris and Euphrates Rivers on the southern end, near the delta that empties into the Persian Gulf.

The Sumerians, as these people came to be called, were most likely the people who remained after the great dispersion of people groups following the Tower of Babel. These people quickly became known for their impressive culture. Their land was fertile because of its location between the two mighty rivers. It was further improved by canals, dams and irrigation systems which channeled water from the rivers into their fields. These people were intelligent and inventive. In fact, we can thank them for the invention of the wheel. They also were the first civilization to use time based on increments of sixty, which we use for our seconds and minutes.

The Sumerians were also the first civilization after the flood that had a written language. They were also diligent in their study of the skies. By studying the moon, they were able to chart months and years and set up a surprisingly accurate calendar. Their writing tool, which was called a stylus, made wedge shaped markings in clay tablets. This type of writing is called cuneiform. There are many written records from the Sumerian civilization.

By reading these clay tablets, historians have uncovered many fascinating pieces of information about the Sumerian's way of life and their belief systems. The Sumerians were polytheists, people who worship many gods. They worshipped the forces of nature that helped or hindered their farming, and they gave high power to the sun, moon and stars. For all of their intelligence and inventiveness, the Sumerians could not have been further from the truth where their gods were concerned.

After the confusing language incident at the Tower of Babel, people groups spread out, starting civilizations in Asia, Africa, and Europe.

The second, large, ancient civilization we will look at is the Ancient Egyptian civilization. After the Tower of Babel, a group of people, thought to be lead by Mizraim, Noah's grandson through his son Ham, went southwest to the northeastern corner of Africa. Here, along the Nile River, they built a massive civilization, which was built on the mighty river because it provided water for the land around it. We are all probably somewhat familiar with the ancient Egyptians with their mummies and pyramids (which we will learn about in our next chapter), but did you know that these people were also accomplished farmers?

Ancient Egyptian farmers were advanced in matters of engineering. They successfully designed and constructed massive irrigation systems to use the water from the Nile River to water their crops. The Nile River is the longest river in the world and is one of the few rivers in the world that runs from south to north. At its northern end, where the water rushes to meet the Mediterranean Sea, the river forms a delta. This delta is one of the most fertile areas on Earth.

The mighty river began to rise to flood levels in June and stayed high through the month of September. Within two to three months the water was back to where it was supposed to be. While the water was high, it was channeled through the irrigation ditches to water the fields. The Nile was also used as a "super highway" to carry goods up to the delta area.

The rise of the Egyptian civilization is estimated to be around 2300 B.C. and is split into three time periods. The first four hundred years, from 2300 through 2000, are called the "Old Kingdom," the next four hundred years, from 1900 through the 1600s B.C., are called the "Middle Kingdom," and the 1500s through the 1300s B.C., are the "New Kingdom."

Narration Break: discuss what you have read in this section. Study it on your map and read "Apologetics through Archaeology" #3.

The Mysterious Civilization of Egypt

Parents: Please pre-read this chapter before reading it to your younger children.

Perhaps the most well-known ancient civilization in history is the Ancient Egyptian civilization. Just like the Sumerians, the Egyptians had a written language. While the Sumerians wrote their wedge-shaped "letters" with a stylus on clay tablets, the Egyptians used a type of paper made from papyrus (pu-PI-rus), a reed that grows along the Nile River. (Papyrus, which is the word from which we derive our word "paper," was also used for woven boats, baskets, shoes and even furniture.) The Egyptians' writing consisted of small pictures drawn to depict a word. This writing is called hieroglyphics, and it has not only been discovered on papyrus scrolls, but also chiseled into the stone walls of palaces and caves.

The Egyptians, like the Sumerians, were polytheists. They depended heavily upon the mighty Nile River to sustain their lives, and they believed the river was controlled by a mighty god. They had hundreds of gods, each with an important job to do. Their kings,or pharaohs, claimed to be gods who had more power than the other, lower gods.

Menes (MEE - neez) was the first true Egyptian king. When the Egyptian civilization first started, the country was divided in half. Menes came from the southern part and conquered the northern part. Menes declared that not only was he the king, but that he was also a god. The

Egyptians feared the gods, so
they did whatever they believed
would make the pharaoh-gods
happy.

The chief of the gods was
Osiris (O-SI-ris). He was the god of
farming and the judge of the
dead. Isis (I-sis) was Osiris's wife,
and their son, Horus (HOR-us),
supposedly had the head of a

Menes United the Southern and Northern Kingdoms. He wore a crown which combined the white and red crowns of both Kingdoms.

falcon. The ancient writings of the Egyptians give much detail about
their belief systems. One of the strange, false beliefs they held was
about the afterlife. They believed that Osiris weighed the heart of the
deceased on a scale. A feather, which represented truth, was placed on
the other side of the scale. If the heart was heavy with sin, a monster
came and ate it up.

It seems strange to us to hear about these people and all of their
gods. We know that God is the one true God, and that He holds all
power, knowledge, and understanding. We know He created all things
and He sent His one and only Son as a sacrifice for our sins. The
Ancient Egyptians did not know about God, though, and so their lives
were spent trying to make all of the various gods happy so they would
not be punished, and so they would have a chance of a happy after-life.

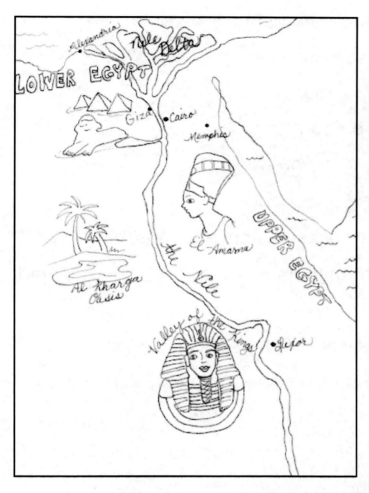

The Ancient Egyptians also held many animals as sacred. We could fill an entire chapter about this subject alone! Animals, which we have as pets, were worshipped and revered in ancient Egypt. Dogs, cats, certain birds, and even a beetle, called a scarab, were thought to be sacred. If anyone killed or abused a sacred animal, that person could be put to death. There are many scriptures describing the culture of Ancient Egypt, and they are interwoven throughout the stories which we will be studying in the weeks to come.

Narration Break: discuss what we have learned so far about the Ancient Egyptians.

As we learned in the first part of this chapter, the Ancient Egyptians were highly superstitious people. Their fear of punishment from one or more of their many gods was much of their motivation in life. The Egyptians had a society based on

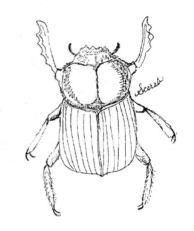

"classes" of people. If you were lucky enough to be born into one of the upper classes, such as priests or soldiers, you might have a more "blessed" life. If you happened to be born to a farmer, shopkeeper, or merchant, then you were stuck in the life of that class. Not many people tried to "move up" to a higher class because they thought that they probably deserved being born into that lower class. This doesn't sound like a very hope-filled life, does it?

One of the most interesting aspects of the Ancient Egyptian culture is how they looked at death. I mentioned earlier that they believed that Osiris was the god who was "judge of the dead." The Ancient Egyptians also held the belief that when they died, their souls stayed close to their

bodies, and because of this, the dead were buried with their most prized possessions. A tomb might contain the deceased's cherished pet, their favorite furniture, jewels, money, and even food! They believed that the soul would return to the body on Judgment Day, so they went to extraordinary lengths to try to preserve the body before burial.

In the beginning of this practice, only the upper class were able to afford to be made into a mummy. This process was extremely long and complicated. After the inner organs, except for the heart, which needed to be weighed against the feather of truth, were removed and placed in jars, the body was soaked ("pickled" really) in a mineral called natron, and wrapped with yards and yards of white cloth. As time went on, even the lower class people were able to mummify their dead. This process, as disgusting as it sounds, was very effective in preserving the bodies of many, many Ancient Egyptians. In fact, many of these mummies have been discovered thousands of years later and placed in museums all over the world.

Another interesting Ancient Egyptian custom related to death was how they were buried. When someone died, that person's family and friends heaped stones on top of the grave. The richer and more prominent the person was, the bigger the pile of stones. Soon, there were kings who each wanted to make sure that his pile of stones was the biggest, and so he started his pile before he had even died. This is how the huge pyramids of Egypt came about. The pyramids were tombs the kings built for themselves before they died.

It has been said that the Egyptian pharaohs were more interested in their lives after death than their lives before death. Even though palatial abodes were built for them while they were living, along with great, huge statues in their likenesses, their real prized accomplishments were their magnificent pyramid tombs. If you think about how buildings are made today, you know that the builders have all sorts of heavy lifting and building equipment such as cranes, backhoes, tractors, and bulldozers. The Ancient Egyptians did not have any of these. They built the pyramids by hand. The huge stones used in the construction of these massive structures were dragged for miles and raised into place by men pushing and pulling on them.

The greatest of these pyramids is called the Great Pyramid. This pyramid was built by a king named Cheops (KEY-ops). It is speculated that this pyramid took one hundred thousand men twenty years to build! Cheops had a huge Sphinx, a statue of a lion with a man's head, built to guard his tomb. This giant statue was to honor the Ancient Egyptian god of the morning. Now, the shifting and blowing sand of the desert has buried the feet of the great Sphinx.

You can visit this spectacular structure even today. There is nothing in the pyramid now, because the mummy of Cheops is not there. After many, many years, the custom of burying the dead with most of their riches became well known all over the world. As the Egyptian civilization declined in its later years, tomb robbers broke into many of the pyramids and stole their contents.

Even though much of the lifestyle and culture of the Ancient Egyptians is well-known around the world, theirs is a history full of

mysticism. Archaeologists have uncovered many detailed writings of their way of life, their belief systems, their family lines and their influence on the world around them. Many of the defining moments of their past are outlined in the Bible, woven throughout the story of God's chosen people.

In our next chapter, we will discover the beginning of the story of the people God called His chosen people, the Israelites and their leader. Much like Noah, this man was chosen to begin a new scene in the history of the world. What a fascinating story he has, too! I hope you are ready to dig in and learn. Get your thinking caps ready; we are going to need them soon.

Narration Break: discuss what you have read in this section. Study it on a world map and read "Apologetics through Archaeology" #4.

Note of interest: Ancient Egyptians were not the only civilizations that mummified their dead. There have been mummies found even in the Americas!

The Calling of Abraham

As we study world history, there is an obvious thread which runs throughout all of the centuries, and that is God's love for mankind. Even though it was human disobedience which brought sin into the world, God had a plan for redemption. This is the story of the man who God chose to become the father of a blessed nation, the nation from which He would one day bring the Messiah, the Savior of the world.

Our story starts in the Middle East, in the land of Sumer, in the city of Ur. Abram (this was his name before God changed it to Abraham) was a decedent of Shem, the son of Noah. His ancestors had been among those who had migrated to the land between the rivers after the flood. Remember, this land is known as the Fertile Crescent because of its ability to grow wonderful crops, and because it is decidedly "moon-shaped." Although those around him were not followers of the One true God, God chose Abram to be a very special person in history.

The Sumerian culture was a busy one. We know, from literally thousands of clay tablets written in cuneiform, that their way of life was extremely busy and industrious. Abram might have been a merchant in Sumer. In Genesis 11: 31-32, it tells the account of how Abram, his wife, Sarai, and Abram's father, Terah, all left Ur and moved north toward the land of Canaan, to live in a city named Haran. It was here that Terah died, and it was also here that Abram received the call to leave Sumer.

We know that when God spoke to him, Abram listened. Abraham would become known as "Father Abraham" to many peoples of the world. The name Abram means "father," while Abraham means "honored father." God changed his name to Abraham and honored him because of his obedience. God also changed Sarai's name to Sarah.

When God came to Abraham and told him to pack up and leave his homeland, Abraham obeyed. God did not tell Abraham where he was to go; He simply said to leave Sumer and to go where God told him.

Abraham and Sarah were without children. The Bible says Sarah was barren, which means that she was unable to have children. This was a big deal in ancient times. People who did not have children were looked down upon by those around them. If you had no children, you must have done something wrong to deserve such a horrible consequence. Many women who could not have children were mocked and scorned by the other women. This is what Sarah had endured for many years.

When God came along and told Abraham to leave Sumer, He also told him that He would make Abraham a "great nation." God was going to make a nation from which He would bring the Savior of all people. How could this be? Abraham, himself, was seventy-five years old at this time, and Sarah was not only barren, she was also old. People did live much longer at this time in history, but still, seventy-five year old Abraham was not considered a young man. So how was God going to make him into a great nation? In Romans 4:3 it says "...Abraham believed God, and it was counted unto him for righteousness."

Abraham and Sarah took Lot, Abraham's nephew, and left the land of Sumer. When they had come to the land of Canaan, God told Abraham that the land he saw around him would be his inheritance and that of his descendants. Moses records this part of the story of Abraham for us in Genesis chapters 12 and 13. Read it carefully, and, on the map provided in the Student's Journal, write down each major move taken by Abraham and Sarah on their journey. Make sure you include the the trip to Egypt in Chapter 13.

🌑 Read Genesis 12 and 13 (The story of the calling of Abraham)

Narration Break: discuss the story of Abraham so far. Complete the above map assignment before moving on.
Parents: please read the note at the end of the chapter now.

As we study the lives of Abraham and his family - often called the Patriarchs - we want to keep an eye on some of the other civilizations of that time. We spent some time in Egypt and Sumer in the last couple of chapters, and now we will turn our eyes to the East. Hanging down into the Indian Ocean, is the almost diamond-shaped country of India. In the ancient times the people, who lived near what is now India, were people of the Indus Valley Civilization. Their civilization was situated in the northwestern part of modern India and the country of Pakistan. Just like the other major civilizations, the Indus Valley Civilization was situated near a major river, the River Indus.

Also like the Sumerians and Egyptians, the people of the Indus Valley had a highly "modernized" civilization. Their streets were wide and straight, and their houses were well built. They even had indoor plumbing! This was accomplished by building the indoor drains to be connected with a large outdoor drain which ran under the street. Archaeologists have discovered many, well-preserved ruins of these cities and have been able to give great details about the early Indus Valley way of life.

The Four Old-World River Valley Cultures

These people are called Ancient Indians, not to be confused with Ancient American Indians. If you have studied American history, you will remember that Native Americans were called Indians by the European explorers who thought they had found a westerly route to India from Europe. The people who they saw - the Americans - were dark in skin color, so they were mistakenly called Indians.

The River Indus, like the Nile in Egypt and the Tigris and Euphrates in Mesopotamia, was a superhighway for the merchants of Ancient India. Archaeologists know that Indus Valley merchants traveled at least as far as Mesopotamia, because some of their pottery and art work have been discovered in Mesopotamian archaeological dig sights. Metals, which are not indigenous to the Indus Valley area, have been found in Indus Valley.

This means that people from the Indus Valley civilization traveled to other parts of the known world.

The people of the Indus River Valley had lived peacefully enough for nearly one thousand years when people from the west invaded their land. Historians are not exactly sure from where these invaders came, but we do know that they were warrior-type people who did not know how to read and write. The invading people took over more and more of India, and just like what usually happens when a country is taken over by a foreign power, little by little the culture changed. Each of the people groups, both the invading peoples and the Indians, adopted some of the others' culture.

Over time, there came to be four distinct castes of people in India. A caste is a class of people. The people in each caste would have nothing to do with the people in the other castes. Each caste had their own types of jobs. For example, the top caste consisted of priests and highly educated people. The next caste down was made up of the rulers and warriors. Farmers and merchants made up the third caste. The fourth and final caste were workers who did the menial jobs and hard labor. What a terrible way to live!

Have you ever heard of Buddhism? This religion was started by an Indian prince named Gautama Buddha (GOU-tu-mu BOO-du). He did not like the caste system and protested it by spending his life trying to ease the suffering of those less fortunate than he. Gautama Buddha, who became known simply as Buddha, taught the people to be kind to each other. People thought he was so good that they worshipped him as a god, therefore starting a religion that would become one of the world's most powerful and widespread religions - Buddhism.

Today, India is extremely crowded with people. The country of India is only one third the size of the United States of America, yet it has more than three times the number of inhabitants. That is a huge number of people, isn't it?

Narration Break: discuss the Indus Valley Civilization and Buddhism. Read through "Apologetics through Archaeology" #5."

Chapter 5

Recommended Bible reading: Genesis 14 - 19 (This is the account of how Abraham and Sarah became impatient and took Hagar, the Egyptian handmaid, and used her for surrogacy, showing disbelief and disobedience concerning God's promise. It also covers the story of the sin and destruction of Sodom and Gomorrah, and the disturbing behavior of Lot's daughters afterward, which led to the beginning of the Moabites and Ammonites.)

Hostility Toward His Brothers

Some conflicts in history die a natural death, while others lay slumbering, waiting to be awakened like an angry colossus. Thus is the story of Abraham, the man chosen to be the father of a special nation. And like so many other great sagas that make up the history of the world, this one is fraught with peril, adventure, sweat, and blood...

In Chapter 5, we met a man who we learned would become the father of a great nation. Through the assigned Bible reading, you learned Abraham, and his wife, Sarah, became impatient for the fulfillment of God's promise. A son was born to Abraham from Hagar, but he was not the promised son. Sometimes we think that one little act of disobedience will not really hurt anyone, but as we are going to see in this chapter of our story, this is exceedingly untrue. This son, Ishmael, who was brought about through Hagar, would prove to be an act of disobedience which still troubles the world today.

Some historical concepts require us to put on our thinking caps and securely tie them under our chin; this is one of those times. We are about to start a two week study about two men. One was born from disobedience and would always carry and live with the knowledge that he was not the chosen one. This insecurity would taint everything in his life and would become the legacy which was passed from one generation to the next. This man would become the "father" of a world religion that is counter to Christianity. The other man was the chosen one; he was the favored son, the father of the chosen nation. His lineage would lead straight to the cross and the way for forgiveness of all mankind.

In our next chapter, we will learn about Isaac, the chosen son, and his descendants, but for now, I want to spend some time with Ishmael, the son born from disobedience. We, as Christians, need to know the history of Ishmael and his descendants, for it is something that still affects us to this day. Before I start the details of Ishmael's descendants, I would like you to go to the next chapter and study the chart of the genealogy of Abraham. Toward the bottom, there is a long, horizontal line with twelve names on it. These are the twelve sons of a man named Jacob, whom you will learn more about in our next chapter. These are the men that became the "fathers" of the twelve tribes of Israel. What I want you to understand is this: Ishmael also had twelve sons.

Genesis 25:12-17 says,

"112 This is the account of the family line of Abraham's son Ishmael, whom Sarah's slave, Hagar the Egyptian, bore to Abraham. 13 These are the names of the sons of Ishmael, listed in the order of their birth: Nebaioth the firstborn of Ishmael, Kedar, Adbeel, Mibsam, 14 Mishma, Dumah, Massa, 15 Hadad, Tema, Jetur, Naphish and Kedemah. 16 These were the sons of Ishmael, and these are the names of the twelve tribal rulers according to their settlements and camps. 17 Ishmael lived a hundred and thirty-seven years. He breathed his last and died, and he was gathered to his people."

As you will learn in our next chapter, Isaac became the grandfather of the twelve sons of Jacob. These tribes became the nation that God had chosen to be the earthly lineage of Jesus Christ, His Son. As you will learn through our study, Satan always tries to counterfeit what God does. The story of Ishmael and his descendants is an extremely clear picture of this. In fact, I believe it is one of the clearest pictures in the Bible depicting this concept.

Before Ishmael was born, the Lord said this about him (Genesis 16:11-12)

"11And the angel of the LORD also said her, you are now pregnant, and you will give birth to a son, and shall call him Ishmael; for the LORD has heard of your misery. 12And he will be a wild donkey of a man; his hand will be against everyone, and everyone's hand against him; and he shall live in hostility toward all his brothers."

I would not want to hear this said about one of my babies, but this is exactly what Ishmael became. As we read in our last chapter's Bible reading, the birth of Ishmael caused much contention between Abraham, Sarah, Hagar, and both of the boys, Ishmael and Isaac. Ishmael and his mother were sent away when Isaac was only a small boy. The Bible makes it clear that Abraham loved Ishmael, and why shouldn't he? Ishmael was his firstborn son. Abraham even begged God to bless Ishmael, but by the time Isaac was old enough to be weaned, probably a toddler, Ishmael was causing trouble. Hagar, Sarah's maid and Ishmael's mother, was sent away, taking her troublesome boy with her.

Genesis 21 (the account of Hagar and Ishmael being sent away)

Narration Break: discuss the story so far.

I hope you have your thinking cap firmly in place, for this is where the story becomes quite intriguing and somewhat complicated. After Hagar and Ishmael were sent away, they returned to the land of Hagar's people - the land of Egypt. There they settled, and Ishmael married a woman of his mother's choosing, from the maidens of Egypt. This was the beginning of a long string of historical happenings...

Ishmael became the unquestioned leader of the desert peoples throughout the Middle East. His descendants settled near the border of Egypt and became Arabian nomads called Bedouins (BED - o - ins). These people groups all had their own gods and belief systems, some sharing gods and idol worship with their neighbors. In other words, they were not any different than the other nations which worshipped many gods.

The development of their own completely separate belief system happened when a man who history calls Mohammed was born in the year 570 A.D. in the city of Mecca. (Islamic tradition states that Ishmael settled in Mecca.) Ishmael had strong family ties in Africa through both Hagar, his mother, and his wife; both of these important women were Egyptian. Even today, there is a colossal stronghold of Islam in Africa.

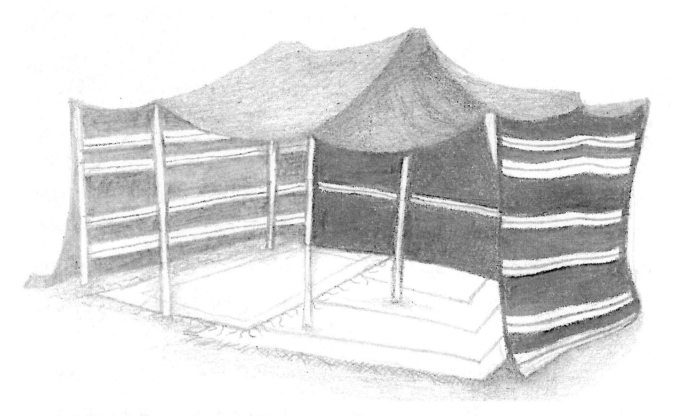

Muslims believe that Mohammed started receiving revelations from Allah in the year 610 A.D. They believe that these messages were communicated through the angel Gabriel. Since they could not deny the birth of Christ, the Muslims turned Him into a prophet to explain Him away, and they chose a verse from John 14 to twist for their use. In John 14:16, Jesus tells His followers that He will send a Comforter (or Counselor). We know that He meant the Holy Spirit, the Spirit of Truth (verse 17). They took verse 16 out of context to say the "prophet" Jesus said there would a final prophet coming that would receive the final revelation. Mohammed was called that prophet.

Mohammed's visions are assembled in a book called the Koran, which is alternately spelled "Quran." It is important for us to know how to pronounce these Arabic pronunciations and meanings: Islam (is-LAM), Allah (al-LAH), and Koran (ko-RON) or Quran (qu-RON). It is also important that, as Christians, we know what makes Islam and Christianity different from each other.

The first important concept to learn is this: we do not share the same God with other religions of the world. Muslims do not believe that Allah is the same as Jehovah. As Christians, we better understand that this is true: **Allah and Jehovah are not the same.** Stick with me as we work through these differences.

Muslims do not and cannot have a personal relationship with their god. In the Koran, there are ninety-nine names for Allah. Not one of those names is personal or close. There is no part of Allah that is relational. There is a line in the Koran that says threateningly "he is as close as your *jugular." Does that sound like our Jehovah - the Great I Am?

While Islam is based on fear and submission, Christianity is entirely based on relationship.

We hold the love, grace, and forgiveness of God as the basis for our beliefs. Jahweh is interested in relationships with each of us. This is why He sent His One and only Son to die for our sins. Sin separated us from His presence. He could not stand that, so He made a way for us to come to Him. His yearning to have a relationship with us is the basis of our faith.

So what does this have to do with Ishmael? All believers of Islam may not be actual descendants of Ishmael, but they all consider themselves to be His spiritual descendants. Does this sound familiar? Remember what I said earlier in the chapter about Satan wanting to counterfeit what God does? As Christians, we are the spiritual descendants of Abraham and his son Isaac.

Another contrast between Islam and Christianity is the certainty of what will follow our time here on Earth. First John 5:12-13 says...

"Whoever has the Son has life; whoever does not have the Son of God does not have life."

We can know! We have security! The followers of Islam have no hope or assurance of eternal security. Mohammed said that he did not know where he was going after he died.

The whole of Islamic belief is based on making Ishmael the inheritor of the promise that God gave Abraham concerning Isaac.  I want you to stop here and read Genesis 22, and when you are finished, come back to read the rest of the chapter in our story.

Who does Genesis 22 say God told Abraham to place on the altar as a sacrifice? In the Koran, Mohammed changed the Biblical happenings on Mount Moriah from Isaac to Ishmael on the altar. If this was true, than everything that was promised to Isaac would actually go to Ishmael.

The "chapters" of the Koran are called suras. In Sura 112 and 3 it says, "Allah, the Eternal, Absolute; he begetteth not, nor is he begotten." Let's compare this to John 3:16-17. The following words are from Jesus, Himself:

"16For God so loved the world, that He gave His one and only Son, that whosoever believes in Him shall not perish, but have everlasting life. 17For God sent not His Son into the world to condemn the world; but to save the world through Him."

In Sura 4, it is written that "they killed him not, nor crucified him." If there was no crucifixion, there is no Savior. This is the number one difference between Islam and Christianity.

Read Genesis 16:11-12 again, and then turn to Genesis 25:18. Compare the two verse segments. What are the similarities? The "he" became a "they." Ishmael's hostility became the hostility that fuels the Islamic religion. Only the good news of our Savior can conquer the darkness of this hostility.

Narration Break: please make sure that you discuss the differences between Islam and Christianity. Read through "Apologetics through Archaeology" #6.

Note of interest...

When we read the Bible, right before we read the book of Psalms, we come upon the story of a man named Job. Most people I know do not care very much for this story, and understandably so, because the story is very sad. Even though we do not know the exact dates of the story of Job, we do know that it took place roughly at the same time as Abraham's call and promise from God. Just because it was placed further into the Old Testament line-up of books, doesn't mean that it took place during the life of King David.

It was Job who cried out in yearning for a Mediator Who would plead his case to God. Read Job 9:32-35. It is this longing for a "bridge" or mediator that fills the souls of the world's lost. We must never turn our backs on the lost and hurting, even the Muslim world. Jesus is the Answer for every person who has or ever will draw breath. He is the only One who can heal the broken hearted.

"We are living history here. Thousands of years have passed, yet the clenched fists of every generation are like links in a chain to the ones behind them. We live in a world where promises and prophecies, that reach all the way back to the book of beginnings, are playing out in part in front of our very eyes. God is our security in turbulent times. Trust Him with all that is in you; trust Him." Beth Moore (2)

*(A predatory animal often attacks its prey by biting this major vein in the neck of its victim.)

The Patriarch and His Sons

After our last chapter, which I am afraid may have been somewhat disturbing for some of our younger readers, I am sure we are ready to turn our eyes to the fulfilled promise of God. Isaac, the son whom God had promised to Abraham and Sarah, was finally born. The name, Isaac, means laughter. I think, perhaps, he was named after the joy that he brought to the family. Isaac did not bring joy to his older brother, Ishmael, however.

When Isaac became old enough to have a wife, Abraham sent his servant back to the country where his extended family lived. He did not want Isaac to marry any of the women from the land in which they had settled. God had the perfect wife for Isaac, and He sent her to meet them. Rebekah was very beautiful, and even better, she was a distant relative of Isaac, which, in those days, was considered a good thing. She agreed to come back to Isaac and become his wife. Isaac and Rebecca had twin sons named Esau and Jacob.

These two may have been twins, but they could not have been more different. Esau, the older brother, was big and burly and had hunting in his blood. He loved to go out into the forest and bring home all sorts of wild game. Isaac loved Esau and the meals of wild game that he made. Jacob was smaller, more gentle, and loved to garden. He had his mother's favor. As the younger of the twins, Jacob was not in line to receive the main portion of his father's blessing. This seemed to bother his mother, Rebekah, more than it did Jacob. She came up with a scheme to trick Isaac, who was quite old by this time, into giving Jacob the blessing. The trick worked, and Jacob received the blessing. He also received a shove out the door! Jacob had to run away from Esau. It would be a long time before Jacob would be able to return.

Jacob wanted to honor his parents' wishes that their sons would not marry a woman from the land of Canaan. Jacob met a beautiful, young woman named Rachel, who he desperately wanted to marry. There was a problem; however, Rachel's father was Laban, Jacob's uncle, and it seemed that scheming ran in the family. Laban told Jacob that he could marry Rachel if he would work  for Laban for seven years. Personally, I think Jacob should have been suspicious, because Laban had a scheme. Jacob loved Rachel so much that he agreed to the seven years of work. Finally the time was over. The bride came in with the veil over her face, which, in those days, was

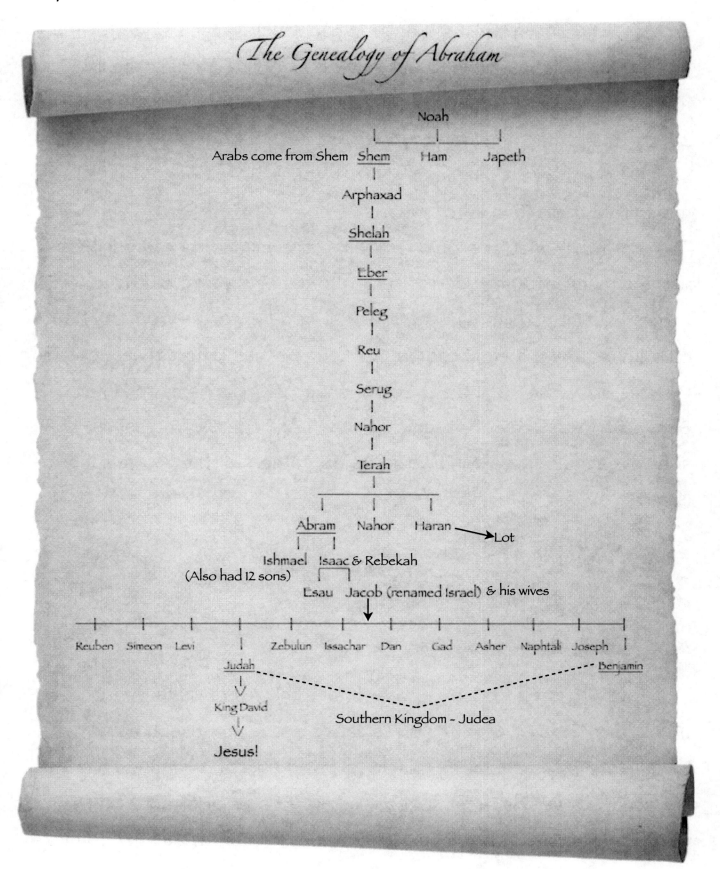

The Genealogy of Abraham

Noah

Arabs come from Shem   Shem   Ham   Japeth

Arphaxad

Shelah

Eber

Peleg

Reu

Serug

Nahor

Terah

Abram   Nahor   Haran ──► Lot

Ishmael   Isaac & Rebekah
(Also had 12 sons)

Esau   Jacob (renamed Israel) & his wives

Reuben   Simeon   Levi   │   Zebulun   Issachar   Dan   Gad   Asher   Naphtali   Joseph   │

Judah - Benjamin

King David

Southern Kingdom - Judea

Jesus!

71

not removed until after the "I do's." When Jacob saw his bride for the first time, he was shocked; it was not Rachel! Back at that time in history, the older sister always got married first, and unfortunately for Jacob, Rachel had an older sister named Leah. So Jacob worked another seven years for Rachel. Now Jacob had two wives, and believe me, this caused him a lot of trouble.

After many years, Jacob's family had grown, and he had become a wealthy man. Jacob decided to return to the land of his mother and father. He met up with Esau, who had married a woman from the house of Ishmael, and the two brothers worked out their differences. Between Genesis 35, verse 20 and 21, God changed Jacob's name to Israel. Study the Genealogy of Abraham on the last page. Do you see all of the sons of Jacob? These sons would be the fathers of the twelve tribes of Israel.

Genesis 27-28 (The account of Rebekah's trick for Jacob to  receive the blessing)

Narration Break: discuss the story so far.

Israel's children were a bit wild. In fact, they were quite the gang of unruly men. Rachel, who had given Jacob two sons, Joseph and Benjamin, died in childbirth. Israel had loved Rachel most and favored her children over his other sons. This caused a lot of discord between the sons, who seethed with jealousy over the unfair treatment. To make

matters worse, Joseph
was a bit of a show off.
The Bible does not tell
us exactly what kind of
young man Joseph was,
but I think it would be
safe to say that he
knew that he was the
favorite one.

 Joseph made his
brothers angry when he
told them about his
frequent dreams. These
dreams always included
imagery of the others
bowing down to him. Of course this made the older brothers boiling
mad.

 One day, Israel gave Joseph a new coat. This was not just any coat,
though; this coat was a masterpiece of color and fine fabric. Joseph was
proud of his new garment and went to show it to his brothers who were
out in the fields. They saw him coming and saw his new coat from a
distance. By the time Joseph reached them, they were angry enough to
kill him. God had His hand on Joseph, though, and in the end, they sold

him to a caravan of Ishmaelites for twenty pieces of silver. Israel was heartbroken when the brothers brought back Joseph's beautiful, new coat drenched in blood along with a tale of how a wild animal had killed Joseph. Little did he know they had soaked the coat in goat's blood, and Joseph was on his way to Egypt as a slave.

Has anything ever happened to you that made you wonder how any good could possibly come from it? I am sure Joseph's mind was reeling from shock as he was led across the hot desert, further and further away from his home and closer to the unknown. Why had God allowed this to happen? What was going to happen? Would he ever see his elderly father again? Would he ever see his home again? He had gone from being the favored son of a Patriarch to a nameless slave boy in one fateful day, but God did have a plan for Joseph.

As we learned in Chapter 4, Egypt was an amazing civilization, with a distinctly different culture than Joseph had ever seen. Upon his arrival in this strange, foreign country, Joseph was sold to Potiphar, who was an important officer of Pharaoh. Over time, Joseph proved himself to be a trustworthy servant, and Potiphar promoted him to a place of great importance in his house and estate. This position was not to last long for Joseph, however, because Potiphar's wife lied about Joseph, and he was thrown into prison.

Can you imagine? As Joseph sat in prison, I am sure that he wondered at this sudden turn of events. What had he done to deserve such a fate? Had he not served God by being honorable and trustworthy in his position at Potiphar's house? Had he not made the most of his slavery? Joseph could have been bitter and angry, but instead, he continued to be honorable and trustworthy.

While Joseph was in prison, there were two other men, Pharaoh's butler and baker, who were incarcerated because Pharaoh was angry at them. These men grew to respect Joseph even though they could not understand why he was so honorable. After all, he had done nothing to deserve his imprisonment. Joseph was respected by the prison guards placed in the position of caring for the other prisoners.

God showed Joseph His presence by helping him to interpret dreams. Both the butler and the baker had dreams for which God gave Joseph the interpretation. When the interpretations came true, the butler was released, and the baker was killed, as their dreams had promised. Joseph asked the butler to remember him in prison, which the butler promised to do and then promptly forgot.

It was not until two years later, when Pharaoh had disturbing dreams, which no one could interpret, that the butler remembered his promise

to Joseph. It was at this time that God brought Joseph out of prison and gave him the meaning of Pharaoh's disturbing dream.

Joseph told Pharaoh the meaning of the dreams. The great land of Egypt was facing seven years of plenty. In these years, the crops would be bountiful, and the land would be more fertile than usual. These would be prosperous years throughout the land. Following these seven plentiful years, however, there would be seven years of extreme want. There would be a drought which would make growing crops impossible. The land would dry up, and the topsoil would blow in great dust storms.

After Joseph told Pharaoh the meaning of the dreams, the grateful king ordered robes of fine linen and the king's very own ring be placed on Joseph. Pharaoh also made Joseph second in command over the entire land of Egypt. Only Pharaoh himself was above him. Take the time now to read this amazing story in the Bible.

Genesis 39 (the story of Joseph in Potiphar's house)

Genesis 41 (the story of the interpretation of Pharaoh's dreams)

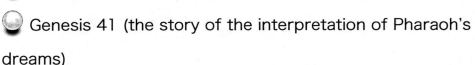

Narration Break: discuss the story of Joseph so far. Read "Apologetics through Archaeology" #7.

The Journey Into Slavery

Joseph was made Pharaoh's Grand Vizier at the age of thirty and was put in charge of preparing the whole nation of Egypt for the impending drought. God showed Joseph how to organize and manage the planting and harvesting of the crops, how to build vast canals to divert the Nile's water into the desert, and how to design and construct vast silos for storage of the crops. At the end of the seven years of plenty came the promised seven years of drought and famine. Archaeologists have found ancient writings describing these years. The drought was so severe that the sands of the desert blew across the land in huge, billowing clouds that blacked out the sun.

The drought and famine was not confined to the land of Egypt; it reached out through the surrounding lands, also. In the land of Canaan, Joseph's family was feeling the effects of the famine. Their crops did not yield any harvest, and their barns were empty. News spread that Egypt had a wise Grand Vizier who had prepared for this drought by storing massive amounts of provisions. In the second year of the famine, Israel heard the news and sent his sons to Egypt to buy enough food to keep them from starving.

Joseph saw them coming and recognized them. I can imagine the flood of memories that came pouring back were not a comfort to him. The last time he had seen his brothers was the day that they had sold him into slavery. The men did not recognize their brother in his Egyptian attire, and they bowed low before him. Joseph remembered the dreams he had when he was a boy, dreams of his brothers bowing to him just as they were now. He gruffly accused them of being spies who had come to see how bad the drought was in Egypt.

The brothers denied this and explained they were the sons of one man from Canaan. They explained that there were twelve sons; one was dead and the other was the youngest son, who was at home with their father. Joseph demanded that they prove what they said by bringing back their youngest brother with them. He also demanded that one of them stay there as a bound servant while the others took some food back home with the command to return with the youngest son.

The brothers spoke amongst themselves saying they were being punished by God for what they did to Joseph so many years earlier. Joseph commanded his servants to place his brothers' money back in the sacks with the corn.

When they returned home, leaving Simeon in Egypt as a ransom, they discovered their gold in the sacks and became even more afraid. Israel was an old man, and his health was not good. He had been so heartbroken over the perceived death of Joseph that he had not been well since that time. Now, when he discovered his youngest son, Benjamin, was to be taken to Egypt to prove that his sons were not spies, he was so heartbroken, he thought he would die!

After their return to Egypt with Benjamin, Joseph commanded that they be brought to his home to dine with him. The brothers were very afraid because they thought for sure they were to be killed or imprisoned by this man who seemed determined to find them guilty of espionage. As they sat at the table, Joseph came in and saw, for the first time in many years, his younger brother, Benjamin. He was so overwhelmed with emotion that he had to excuse himself to his bed chamber to cry.

Again, Joseph sent his brothers back with corn and grain, and, again, he ordered their money be placed in their bags. This time, however, he ordered his servants to follow them. When his brothers had gone a short distance, the servants stopped them and brought them back to Joseph. The brothers' bags were searched, and out from each bag, fell

the gold coins. The brothers were so distressed that they fell to the ground in complete despair.

It says in Genesis 45 Joseph could not refrain himself anymore. He cried out for everyone to leave him alone with these men who he had framed as spies and thieves. Once all of his servants were gone from the room, he wept loudly and told his brothers who he really was. I can imagine they thought this Egyptian man was crazy. Joseph, in his full Egyptian ruler attire, which probably included heavy eye makeup and a black wig, was not even remotely familiar to them. They had given up all hope of ever seeing their younger brother, who they had sold into slavery. The image of his forlorn face, drooping shoulders, and bound hands, as he walked away across the desert... this was the image which was burned into each of their minds. Now, here this man stood, saying that he was Joseph. How could it be?

Genesis 43 - 44 (The account of the brothers' trips to Egypt)

Narration Break: discuss the story of Joseph brothers' journeys to Egypt. Why do you think Joseph didn't just tell his brothers who he was right away?

Joseph spoke again. This time, he reassured his brothers that God

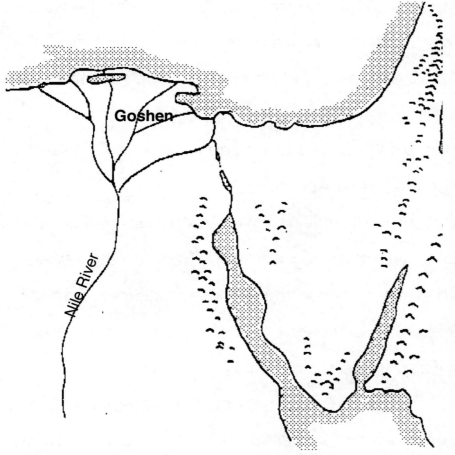

Himself had sent him to Egypt. He begged his brothers not to be angry with themselves for selling him into slavery. What they had intended for evil, God had used to save them all from starvation. What a reunion they had!

Pharaoh heard that Joseph's family had

come from Canaan, and he made an offer that would change the course of history. He told Joseph to tell his father, all of his brothers, their wives, and their children to come and live in Egypt. Pharaoh, himself, would provide the wagons and oxen to bring back the family. Pharaoh promised he would give them a separate section of land. This land was good for growing crops and would support the whole family. This land was called Goshen, and it was prime real estate near the Nile Delta.

Joseph's brothers rushed home to tell their father the wonderful news. Joseph was alive and well! He was a powerful ruler in Egypt, with a family of his own. Israel and his sons and grandchildren packed up everything they owned and started the journey to Goshen. On the way, they stopped to rest for the night at a place called Beersheba. Here God appeared to Israel in a dream and told him not to be afraid to go to Egypt. God told him He would be with them and make them a great nation. The Lord also told Israel He would bring them back to Canaan, the land which had been promised to Abraham.

It was in this way that Joseph's family, the Children of Israel, came to live in Egypt. There were many of them by this time. Each of the twelve brothers had children, and some of those children had children. Genesis 46:27 says there were "three score and ten," including the two sons of Joseph who were born in Egypt. This means there were seventy members in the family. When Joseph heard that his family was coming into Egypt, he ordered his chariot be prepared so he could go and meet his father. What a happy reunion this was. Joseph and his father embraced and wept; neither of them had thought they would ever see the other again.

The family of Israel were shepherds by occupation. Joseph, who was very wise to the traditions and opinions of Egypt, warned his father and brothers to be a shepherd was considered an "abomination unto the Egyptians." Therefore, he said, they must say that they were traders of cattle if anyone, especially Pharaoh, asked them what their occupations were.

The famine continued for five more long years, and people from far and wide came to Egypt to buy grain. Little by little Joseph bought up cattle and land in exchange for seed, corn, and grains. By the end of the famine, the nation of Egypt had vast holdings of wealth. The family of Joseph prospered in the land of Goshen, while the surrounding areas were still suffering from the effects of the famine.

Seventeen years passed, and the Children of Israel grew in number. By now, Israel had grown exceedingly old; his years were one hundred forty-seven. Before he died, Israel called Joseph to him. Joseph brought his two sons with him, and Israel stretched out his hands to bless them. Turn to the genealogy of Abraham in Chapter 7, and look at the line of Israel's sons. Can you see that Joseph's sons replaced him in the line of tribes? Joseph passed his place in the family onto his two sons.

At the end of this chapter, you will read Israel's blessing over all of his sons. In those days, it was tradition for the father to pass down blessings and benedictions to his children. What a wonderful tradition! This is what God has called all parents to do for their children. It is their responsibility to train them in the way they should go and to remember the "landmarks." Landmarks are monumental happenings in each of our Christian lives and walks. In Deuteronomy 6:4-9 it says:

"4 Hear, O Israel: The Lord our God, the Lord is one. [a] 5 Love the Lord your God with all your heart and with all your soul and with all your strength. 6 These commandments that I give you today are to be on your hearts. 7 Impress them on your children. Talk about them when you sit at home and when you walk along the road, when you lie down and when you get up. 8 Tie them as symbols on your hands and bind them on your foreheads. 9 Write them on the door frames of your houses and on your gates."

The recalling of these landmarks is exactly what passes the love of Jesus from one generation to the next. We are always only one generation away from forgetting; we must determine not to be that forgetful generation.

After Israel had passed on, Joseph had his father's body embalmed, and he and his brothers carried it back to Canaan, as Israel had asked. There they buried him in a cave tomb, where Abraham and Sarah, Isaac and Rebecca, and Leah had all been buried. After the funeral, the brothers returned to their families in Goshen.

Joseph lived to be one hundred ten years old, and when he died, his family embalmed his body and placed it in a coffin. He had requested that he be buried in Canaan with his father and grandfathers, as Israel had done. All of his brothers were dead, along with that entire generation. Their children and their grandchildren grew in number until they were a mighty people. Exodus 1:7 says...

"7 but the Israelites were exceedingly fruitful; they multiplied greatly, increased in numbers and became so numerous that the land was filled with them."

By this time, the kindly Pharaoh, who had been Joseph's friend, had long been gone, and the attitude of the Pharaoh, who was now on the Egyptian throne, was not favorable toward the Children of Israel. In fact, this Pharaoh was afraid because the Israelites, as they were called now, had grown to be such a mighty people. He decided to enslave them and afflict them with the burden of building treasure cities and tombs for him.

He also tried to keep them from multiplying by commanding that the boy children born to the Israelites all be killed. Exodus 1:17 says the midwives, whom the Pharaoh had commanded to destroy the baby boys, feared God and did not do as the king had commanded. When the children of Israel still multiplied and grew in number, the Pharaoh commanded that any Egyptian, who saw an Israelite boy child, destroy the child by throwing him into the Nile River. God had a plan for these people, though. He was going to raise up a deliverer from amongst them to lead them back to the land He had promised Abraham.

 Exodus 2 - 3 (The story of Moses)

Narration Break: discuss the rest of the story of how Joseph's family came to Egypt. Read "Apologetics through Archaeology" # 8.

Point of interest...

Genesis 14:13 is the first place the word "Hebrew" is used. Abraham is called "Abram the Hebrew." The term "Semites" or "Semitics" comes from the offspring of Shem, the son of Noah.

Hammurabi of Babylon

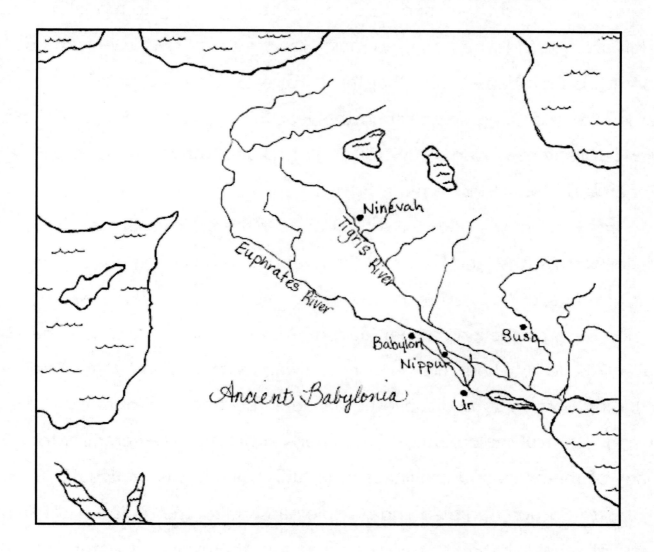

We are going to take a short detour from our story of God's chosen people and turn our attention back to the west. The land between the Tigris and Euphrates Rivers at the southern end had become known as Babylon. This land, which we called Sumer in Chapter 3, had endured a rather chaotic existence so far. Way back around the year 2300 B.C., a king named Sargon (SAR-gone) had tried to unite the Sumerians.

This king was not a good man; he used force to make people behave the way he thought they should. Perhaps he was trying to model his reign after a king who had lived many years ago in Egypt. We learned about this Egyptian king in Chapter 4. To refresh our memories, remember that, long ago, around the year 3000 B.C., this Egyptian king, Menes (also called Narmer [NAR-mer]), had united the then-divided Upper and Lower Kingdoms of Egypt.

King Sargon was determined to conquer the entire area of Mesopotamia (the land between the rivers), and he accomplished this by fighting every city-state located here. Eventually, he defeated them all and became the king as he desired. He then built a city which he called Akkad (AH-kad). His new empire was called Akkadia (ah-KAY-dee-uh). King Sargon soon discovered he would have to continue to use his army to control the conquered members of his Akkadian empire, for many of the cities and provinces did not like him or his tactics...

After Sargon had died and his rule had ended, the region had fallen back into their old habit of fighting amongst themselves. Centuries had passed and still, there was no peace to speak of.

All the kings since Sargon had not been able to unite the city-states of Mesopotamia. Many of them had given up and settled for being king of parts of the land. Some of them tried to use force to make the people obey, and they soon found out how fierce the kings of the city-states could be. Most of them did nothing to make a lasting change for the good. Fast-forward to the year 1792 B.C., and a king named Hammurabi (ham-u-ROB-ee) was on the Babylonian throne. Hammurabi had inherited, from his father, the rather dubious job of being king of Babylon.

Hammurabi was a different type of king than his predecessors; he wanted the people to obey him because they wanted to. He wanted to

be a just and fair king, who listened to the troubles of his people. This was a novel concept to the people of Babylon, so Hammurabi had to find a way to prove what he said was really how he wanted things to be. How could he do this?

Hammurabi decided to make a new set of laws for his people. These laws would be just and fair. He wanted his entire kingdom to follow the same rules. Of course, the Babylonians

did not worship the One True God, so
Hammurabi attributed his new laws to the
sun-god, Marduk (MAR-duck). He had his
list of two hundred eighty-two laws
engraved on huge stone pillars. These
laws are called the Code of Hammurabi.

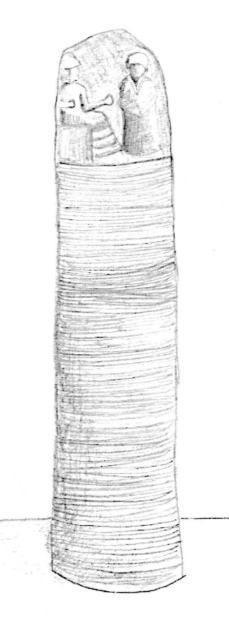

Narration Break: discuss the story so far.

The laws were prefaced with these
words...
"Anu and Bel called by name me, Hammurabi,
the exalted prince, who feared Marduk, the chief
god of Babylon, to bring about the rule in the
land."
Some of these laws are listed below.

- If someone cuts down a tree on someone else's land, he will pay for it.
- If someone is careless when watering his fields, and he floods
  someone else's field by accident, he will pay for the grain he has
  ruined.
- If a man wants to throw his son out of his house, he has to go to a

judge and tell him he doesn't want his son living with him anymore. The judge will decide if the reasons are good or not. If the judge does not think the reasons are good, the man cannot throw out the son.

- If the son has done some great evil to his father, the father must forgive him the first time. But if he does evil again, the father can throw him out.

- If a thief steals a cow, sheep, donkey, goat, or pig, he will pay ten times what it is worth. If he doesn't have the money to pay, he will be put to death.

- An eye for an eye, and a tooth for a tooth. If a man puts out the eye of another man, put his own eye out. If he knocks out a tooth, knock out his own tooth.

- If a doctor operates on a patient, and the patient dies, the doctor will have his hand cut off.

- If a builder builds a house and the roof collapses, and the owner dies, the builder will be put to death.

- If a robber breaks a hole in the wall of a house to break in and steal, he should be put to death in front of the hole in the wall.

So, you may be asking, "What's the big deal about a list of laws written by some guy named Hammurabi?" Actually, there are two reasons that Hammurabi's Code is important. The first reason is this is the first written set of laws that we know of. These laws give us a peek into the lives of the early Babylonians. What kind of society would live by these codes? Many of these laws pertain to the moral and cultural aspect of the society.

The second, and perhaps even more important reason is, these codes applied to all of the citizens of Babylon. Nobody was exempt from them. This means rich people, as well as poor people, were held to the same level of honesty. Compared to the other civilizations of that time, these laws were very unique.

Hammurabi was extremely religious. He gave the gods credit for giving him all of his "wonderful" laws, and he encouraged his people to learn from the gods. He also rebuilt the temples and sacred sights which had been destroyed in the years of war between the city-states. Little did he know that many centuries later, Babylon would become one of the most powerful nations on the face of the earth.

The reign of Hammurabi lasted forty-two years from 1792 to 1750 B.C., but a stone engraved with his set of laws still exist. A stele (an engraved, upright stone monument) containing the Code of Hammurabi was found by an Egyptologist, named Gusave Jéquier, in the year 1901. It had been taken as plunder as far back as the 12th century B.C. to Susa, Elam, which is modern day Khuzestan, Iran.

This giant artifact is shaped like a huge index finger. The engravings of the Code are written in the Akkadian language using cuneiform. There are forty-four columns of writing, containing twenty-eight paragraphs. It is considered to be one of the world's oldest deciphered writings of noteworthy length. You may be able to see it one day, because it is in the Louvre, a famous museum in Paris, France.

Babylon, the land between the rivers, and the original home of Abram, renamed Abraham, would eventually play an important role in the history of the Hebrews. In our next chapter, we will return to the story of the family of Israel. God is about to lead them out of slavery and back to the land which He had promised to Abraham's offspring.

Narration Break: discuss Hammurabi's Code of laws. What do you think of them? Do you think that they are fair? Read "Apologetics through Archaeology" #9.

The Plundering of Egypt

Have any of you ever seen a bush that was on fire, but was not being consumed by the flames? We learned, in our Bible reading at the end of Chapter 8, that Moses had run away after killing an Egyptian taskmaster. He had been living as a shepherd for forty years, when God appeared to him. God had an important assignment for Moses; do you remember what it was? Did Moses want to obey? What was his excuse?

While Moses was out in the plains of Midian, his people were still being oppressed by the Egyptians. The Bible says God heard their groaning and "remembered" the promise which He had made to Abraham. When it says "remembered," it does not mean that God had forgotten the Israelites; it simply means that He knew the time of deliverance was coming. He knew where Moses was, and it was time to deliver the message that he was the one chosen to lead his people out of slavery.

Chapter 10

God also knew Moses was nervous about speaking. Maybe Moses stuttered, or maybe he simply did not want to confront Pharaoh, with whom he had shared his childhood. Either way, God made a provision for him. I love how God does not hold our weakness against us. He knows we are human, and humans have downfalls. Even though He knows about our weakness, He does not let us use it as an excuse for disobedience. When He tells us to do something, He does not expect us to do it in our own strength; He gives us His grace and strength to do it. This is just what He did for Moses, and He sent Moses's older brother, Aaron, to be his helper.

Moses told his wife and family that he was being sent back to Egypt, and then he set off toward the land of his birth. On his way, he met up with Aaron, just as God had told him he would. Together, the brothers went to Egypt and asked for audience with Pharaoh. The Bible does not go into a great amount of detail about this meeting, but I can imagine it was somewhat surreal for Moses. What happened next went down as one of the most amazing displays of God's power in all of history.

God told Moses He was going to harden Pharaoh's heart, so he would not want to let the slaves go. He also told Moses that He was going to show His power by inflicting the people of Egypt with plagues, which would destroy vast amounts of the Egyptians' riches. God did this to show His own power over the most powerful civilization of that day.

As we learned in previous chapters, the Egyptians were polytheists - worshippers of many false gods. Study the list of the ten chief gods of the Egyptians. Note especially over what element of power each god was believed to have dominion. Why did I list the ten chief false gods of

---

The Ten Chief False gods of Egypt

1. Hapi: the god of the Nile River, was depicted as a "water bearer."

2. Heka: the god of renewal, had the head of a frog

3. Geb: god of the earth, was depicted as being over the "dust of the earth."

4. Khepri: god of creation and movement of the sun, had the head of a fly.

5. Hathor: the goddess of love and protection, had the head of a cow.

6. Isis: goddess of medicine and peace.

7. Nut: goddess of the sky.

8. Seth: god of storms and disorder.

9. Ra: the god of the sun.

10. Last, but certainly not least: Pharaoh, who was considered to be the ultimate power of Egypt.

#1 Water to blood

#2 Frogs everywhere

#3 Gnats came out
of the ground

#4 Flies everywhere

#5 Sick livestock

a heathen nation? We will soon see how God specifically sent destructions to these gods.

Just as God had said, He hardened Pharaoh's heart, and Pharaoh would not let the Israelites go. God's judgment was brought against the land of Egypt. Plague after plague swept through the land, and only the land of Goshen, where the Hebrews lived, was spared.

Time after time, Pharaoh told Moses and Aaron to stop the effects of the plagues, and he would let their people go. Time after time, the plague would stop, and Pharaoh's heart would be hardened. Ten times, the Israelites cried out in agony. Would God really deliver them? Finally, the tenth plague came. The land lay barren, ravaged by

#6 Boils and sores

#7 Hail and fire

#8 Locusts come from
the sky

#9 The sky was dark

#10 Death of the
first born

the effects of the plagues, which had stripped the land of all of its

productivity.

Study the following chart of the ten plagues.

The Ten Plagues Against Egypt

Plague #1: God instructed Moses to touch the Nile River with his rod. The water turned to blood.

Plague #2: Frogs by the tens of thousands, came up out of the water.

Plague #3: Gnats came up out of the dust of the earth.

Plague #4: Swarms of flies came and tormented people and livestock alike. The flies spread disease and sickness.

Plague #5: Death of livestock and cattle.

Plague #6: Boils and sores

Plague #7: Hail and fire storms came from the sky and destroyed the land

Plague #8: Locusts came from the sky, darkening the sky.

Plague #9: The sky was completely dark, and the sun was blotted out.

Plague #10: Death to the firstborn. Even Pharaoh's own firstborn son, heir to the throne, was killed.

Now, go back to the chart of the ten chief Egyptian gods. Compare

them one by one; do you see the pattern? Can you see how God used

each of the plagues to specifically conquer the gods of the land?

Chapter 10

Exodus 4 (The account of God's conversation with Moses, commanding him to go to Egypt.)

Narration Break: discuss the story so far.

There is historical and archaeological evidence that these plagues, which are outlined in the book of Exodus, brought long-lasting effects to the land of Egypt. The land was stripped bare by the storms. Crops were destroyed by hail, firestorms, and locusts. The detestable stench of rotting livestock and frogs filled the land. Dead flies and gnats everywhere added to the general atmosphere of death. How awful to witness a land, so brought to ruin, by the very hand of God.

While the plague of death swept through the land of Egypt, God had provided a means of protection for the Israelites. He gave them specific instructions they had to follow. Read this story in Exodus before moving on.

Exodus 11 - 12 (The account of God's protection of the Israelites during the plague of death.)

When this final and most horrible plague had swept through the land, it left in its wake a wailing which filled every home in Egypt. By far, the deaths of the firstborn children were the most horrific outcome of all of the plagues. God had successfully put a stop to the most affluent civilization on the earth at that time. It was on this scene that Pharaoh gazed down upon, and a loathing for the Hebrew people filled his being. He called Moses to him and told him to take his people and leave Egypt.

Chapter 10

It says in Exodus 12 that the Hebrews left in huge numbers, six hundred thousand men, not counting the women and children. All together, there were well over two million Israelites who marched out of Egypt that day. On their way out, the Hebrews took riches from Egypt. Exodus 12:36 says the Egyptians gave them everything that they asked for. It was in this way that the Israelites "spoiled" or plundered the Egyptians. These jewels and riches would later be used in a special place which was specifically for worshipping God - the Temple.

When I was a child, I read Bible stories about the Israelites when they were slaves in Egypt. I did not understand why God would allow His chosen people to be slaves for all of these years. If He loved them, why did He allow them to go through so much pain? It was not until later that I learned about all of the wars fought in the land of Canaan and the surrounding areas, during those four hundred years of slavery in Egypt. God had protected His chosen people by keeping them safe in Egypt. They had gone in as a family of seventy people, but they came out as a nation of nearly three million, a nation strong enough to survive.

God was going to lead the Children of Israel back to the land, which He had promised to Abraham. When God gives a promise, He always keeps it. After God had led His people out of Egypt, you would think they would be eager to do everything He told them to do, but this was not the case. Over and over, the Israelites did not trust Him. Over and over, they did not obey Him. God gave the Israelites a set of ten laws called the Ten Commandments. These laws were to protect the Hebrews from their own unbelief and distrust. These laws are a sound moral code for all people, even those of us who live thousands of years later.

It is wonderful to know God knows everything. He is the same yesterday, today, and forever. We should trust and obey Him because He knows what is best for us. The Bible says that He is near to those who trust Him. God also did this for His chosen people.

We have read many chapters from the books of Genesis and Exodus, which outline our story so far. The next book of the Bible, Leviticus, gives a greatly detailed account of the laws that God gave the Israelites. These laws had a lot to do with how and what they were supposed to eat and not to eat. There were many types of meat which were considered to be unclean. Now that we know about the microscopic world around us, we know about germs, bacteria, and even little, tiny parasites, but at that time, these were all unknown dangers.

God told the Children of Israel not to eat animals that had divided hooves but did not chew their cuds. Pigs were such animals. Why would God tell them not to eat these animals? We now know animals that do

not chew their cuds are much more susceptible to parasites than animals who do chew their cuds. So God told the Israelites to only eat animals that had divided hooves <u>and</u> chewed their cuds. This eliminated the threat of sickness through parasites. While people groups all around them were dying from sickness and plagues spread by these animals, the Hebrews were safe.

⬤ (Optional) Joshua 6 (The account of how God delivered the city of Jericho into the hands of the Israelites.)

Chapter 10

Narration Break: discuss the story of how God delivered the Israelites from Pharaoh. Read "Apologetics through Archaeology" #10.

Interesting notes: 1.) Back in the time period which we are studying, people did not know much about medicine or how the body works. The Ancient Egyptians were more medically advanced than other civilizations, because they experimented with different herbs and procedures. For example, they knew that moldy bread, when laid on an open sore, helped the body to heal and not become infected; however, they did not know why this worked, because they did not know about bacteria. The Egyptians could also do minor surgeries and even set broken bones.

2.) The Bible gives a detailed account of what happened after God brought them out of Egypt. I have included the readings which show specific "snap shots" of certain historical times and happenings. However, I cannot assign all of the Biblical chapters which would flesh out the details; that would entail reading entire books of the Bible. If you, as a parent, or your older, motivated high school student would like to read these books of the Bible, please do so! The reading would greatly enhance the study.

An Ancient Civilization Backdrop

Christian historians estimate that there were approximately 5,000 years between Creation and the birth of our Savior, Jesus Christ. As you may imagine, in those thousands of years, there were many civilizations that rose and fell. Some of these left surprisingly good records, while others have disappeared without a trace. There have been many, thick, dusty volumes written detailing past civilizations. We do not have room in this book for even half of these, so we will focus on the main civilizations which helped form the history of the ancient world.

In this chapter, we are going to look at a few of these civilizations. Some of the civilizations fell into ruin, while others morphed into nations which are still around today.

The Bible is full of strange names... Assyrians, Phoenicians, Hittites, and Philistines. Some of the names are hard to wrap our tongues around, aren't they? What were these people like? What kinds of civilizations did they have? The Bible tells us about some of them in great detail and how they affected the world and the Israelites.

Chapter 11

Do you remember the story of a Babylonian king, named Hammurabi, in Chapter 9? Hammurabi ruled his kingdom in the lower part of the land between the rivers. He was a relatively good king who had a code of laws under which everyone was treated equally. To the north of Hammurabi's kingdom was another kingdom, ruled by another man. This king of North Mesopotamia was named Shamshi-Adad (SHAM-shee ah-DAD). Shamshi-Adad was not like Hammurabi. He believed in force, and he was extremely brutal to his subjects if they did not obey him. Shamshi-Adad became ruler by taking over the northern part of Mesopotamia by force.

Shamshi-Adad ruled his kingdom from his "capital city" of Assur (AS-sur), and soon, he and his people were called Assyrians (a-SEER-ee-ins). If you have read many Old Testament stories, you may have heard this name. The Children of Israel had many battles with these people, and so did many other nations. So how did these people live? Like the other civilizations of the time, the Assyrians were polytheists. Their two main gods were Ashur and Ishtar. The Assyrians had inherited the language of their ancestors, the Sumerians. They had libraries that contained "books" of clay tablets. You are probably somewhat familiar with the name of Assyria's capital city, Nineveh. (You can read about this city in the book of Jonah.) Nineveh was renowned for its extensive library.

Shamshi-Adad gave his kingdom to his two sons before he died. These two sons did not get along, and instead of strengthening their father's kingdom, they fought and weakened Assyria. Hammurabi saw the opportunity to take over, and marched north. One by one, he began taking over the cities of the Assyrian Empire. One of these cities was Mari. (There is some interesting information about this city in the "Apologetics through Archaeology" section for this chapter.) After Hammurabi took over Assyria, he did not kill all of the Assyrian leaders. Instead, he let them stay and rule under his supervision. As long as they followed his code of laws, he let them stay in peace. In this way, the Assyrians were able to maintain their identity at some level and would remain very much a separate empire until their ultimate fall in the early 600's B.C.

The Bible has a lot to say about the Assyrians. There are many accounts of them taking over various lands and destroying the people who lived there. They used whatever means they deemed necessary to overrun cities. The Assyrians were notorious for their cruelty to the peoples they conquered, and they demanded a high price from those they left alive. Time and time again, the Assyrians came against the nation of Israel. God delivered His people from the Assyrians many times, but, as you will learn a little later, there came a time in which He let the Assyrians divide and conquer them.

2 Kings 19: 17

(An account of how Assyria took over ten of the twelve tribes. This even happened a bit later in the chronological flow of our story, but it is a good example of the Assyrians in the Bible.)

Narration Break: discuss the story of the Assyrians.

Another civilization the Children of Israel came across were the Phoenicians. These people were known for their fine pottery, shipbuilding, sailing, and glass-blowing. Have you ever seen someone blow glass? It is an amazing process in which the glass maker literally makes glass "bubbles" with melting-hot glass. While the glass is hot, it can be molded into astounding shapes, and when it is cool, the blown glass is beautiful and shiny. This was the most valuable of all glass products in ancient times.

Another extremely valuable Phoenician product was purple dye. The dye-makers had a well guarded secret of boiling Murex snails to make this rich, purple dye. It was a stinky process, but cloth dyed in this royal purple color sold for extravagant prices. Kings of every civilization wore

their robes of royal purple... snail purple!

The Phoenician merchants traveled the Mediterranean Sea with their ships laden with merchandise and settled, not only in Canaan, but also along the northern edge of Africa and the southern tip of what is now Spain. These people got along with the Israelites for the most part; they intermarried with the Hebrews, and they traded with each other.

In the land, which we now call Turkey, there once lived a tribe of people who are mentioned in numerous Bible verses - the Hittites. At this time in history, the area was called Anatolia (ana-TOLE-ia). Historians are not positive of the origins of this people group. They were probably a group of people who shared a common language after the Tower of Babel and wandered into this area around 2000 B.C.

The Hittites were polytheists, who carved their gods into rock surfaces. They were aggressive people, who declared war on anyone living within a thousand miles of them, especially Egypt. This went on for many years until, finally, they made a peace treaty and sealed it with an arranged marriage. In 1270 B.C., the Egyptian Pharaoh Ramesses II married a Hittite princess. This finally brought some peace, and, as written records show, the two civilizations influenced each other in a more positive way.

When a warring tribe from the Mediterranean Islands came into Anatolia, they conquered the Hittites and destroyed most of their cities and dwellings. Some of the Hittites escaped and moved into what is now Syria. They lived here until the Assyrians took over that region.

Now, let us move a little to the east, to what is now the country of Greece. In the ancient days of history, there was a rather mysterious group of people living there. It was not until the late A.D.1800's that anyone knew about these people. We do not know what they called themselves, but there are enough artifacts to give a small glimpse into their lifestyle. We know they had beautifully carved statues, pottery, and jewelry.

We call these people Mycenaeans (my-SIN-e-uns), because their civilization was discovered close to the city of Mycenae in Greece. Because of this, these people are considered to be early Greeks. We will learn more about the Greek civilization in a later chapter because it is considered to be one of the most prominent ancient civilizations. It is important to know that the Mycenaeans were a vital power. Even though there is not as much known about them, they did have an important role in the early commerce between the civilizations of that time.

Situated on a fertile strip of land, which borders the Mediterranean Sea, there lived a people group called the Philistines. When the Children of Israel marched back into the Promised Land, little did they know that this tribe of people would become the most bothersome of all neighbors. It was the Philistines (FIL-u-steens) who would declare war against God's people and dare them to send their mightiest soldier to fight their most powerful warrior.

We will learn about this event in a later chapter. For now, it is important to know what kind of people the Philistines were. They were fearsome warriors, and their control over the local iron trade made their enemies tremble. Their weapons were stronger than any others, and they were skilled soldiers.

Narration Break: narrate what you have learned while you study the map project in your Student's Journal pages. Read "Apologetics through Archaeology" #11.

Ancient China

A couple thousand years after the dispersion of people following the Tower of Babel, there were people groups creating civilizations on all seven continents. The people groups who we studied in our last chapter lived in what they considered as the the "center of the world." This area, which we call the Middle East, was the hub of activity at that time. The Middle Eastern civilizations thought the Indus Valley people were distant and somewhat strange, and the people who lived even further east were thought to be immensely mysterious.

Like most civilizations of the ancient times, the early civilizations in Asia and Africa started along major rivers. The rivers served as a source of water for crops and a "super highway" for trade boats. Like Mesopotamia, nestled between the Tigris and Euphrates Rivers and the Indus Valley civilization beside the River Indus, the early Chinese civilization also first developed between two rivers. The land between the Yellow River and the Yangtze River is called the Yellow River Valley. The land here is rich and fertile, perfect for farming.

Chinese farmers grew many of the same crops and raised many of the same animals that other farmers of other civilizations grew at that time, but they had something that no one else had - rice.

For many years, the Chinese civilization consisted of numerous small farming communities and villages, all spread out from each other. There was no true unity as a tribe or nation. It was when a man, named Huang Di (hwang-DEE), became ruler, that the small towns and provinces were united.

There are not many written historical accounts of this man's life, although there are many legends! This was before the Chinese people had a written language, so whatever accounts we have were handed down from one generation to the next. No one knows for certain how much of it is true and how much has become legend.

Some details we do know are that around the time of Huang Di, the Chinese used metals to make tools and statues, and the most commonly used metal was bronze. Archaeologists have found many beautiful, ornate, bronze pots and vases. The Ancient Chinese were superstitious, and like the Ancient Egyptians, they held some fanciful ideas about the afterlife. When a nobleman died, animals and even servants were sacrificed to be buried with their master, so they could serve him in the afterlife. They also believed that their ancestors became gods, who they needed to appease with gifts and worship. The Shang (CHANG) Dynasty began when a man named T'ang (TANG) came to power. When one family rules generation after generation, this is called a dynasty. The Shang family ruled China for five hundred fifty years. When you work on the timeline project for this chapter, you will see how the history of Ancient China is divided into these dynasties.

Many legends about the Ancient Chinese abound! One legend in particular has become quite famous, and this is the legend of Huang Di's wife, Lei Zu (lay-TZU). This legend explains how a moth's cocoon became the origin of a huge Chinese industry - silk!

The Legend of the Silk Worm

Once upon a time, in the land of the Ancient Chinese, a lady - the wife of the emperor himself - was taking her tea and lunch in her garden. It was a lovely day, and Lei Zu was enjoying the warm breeze and the birds' songs. As her servant poured her tea, she smiled expectantly. She loved to eat in her garden under the mulberry trees, where everything smelled so delightful at this time of year.

Lei Zu accepted her tea cup delicately and was just lifting it to her lips, when something plopped into her tea!

"Oh, goodness!" the empress exclaimed.

"What is it, my lady," the servant asked.

"Something has fallen into my tea... wait! Oh my! It is a cocoon...what is it doing? Look!" The empress carefully removed the cocoon from her tea and gasped. All thoughts of her lunch and tea were dismissed, as she carefully unraveled yard after yard of thin, shimmering thread from around the moth inside the cocoon.

As the empress and her maid unraveled the silken thread, they walked around the garden with the cocoon thread draped here and there.

When they finally reached the end, they gasped as the air-light thread glimmered and shone in the sunlight. It was truly the most beautiful thread they had ever seen.

When the empress had her dressmaker weave the thread into cloth, the results were a nearly weightless, shimmery fabric which made gorgeous clothing. Lei Zu then had the material made into a robe for her husband, the emperor.

The making of silk became a closely guarded secret. Eventually, this mysterious material became a highly coveted Chinese export, and the silk industry became extremely important to China. The caterpillars, which produced the silk, were grown and fed mulberry leaves until they spun their cocoons. The cocoons were then soaked in hot water to loosen the strands of precious, silken thread. The lowly silk worm became an important part of Chinese history.

Narration Break: discuss the story so far.

The first Chinese written language was what we refer to as pictographs; in other words, each symbol stood for an object. The Ancient Chinese pictographs were engraved on bone, rock, or metal. By studying these early writings, historians can learn more about the culture and how the writing has changed over the centuries. Chinese writing is still a type of pictographs, although it has evolved into a more typical written language. Today, Chinese characters are written in calligraphy (cu-LIG-ru-fy).

We learn, from these ancient writings, that family was an important aspect of Chinese life. Many generations lived together, and older people were highly respected. Grandparents held a high place of honor in the home. Children were taught from a very young age that it was their responsibility to take care of their parents when they became old or sick. Families spent many hours together, enjoying a variety of recreational activities. The Chinese loved to play together. There were festivals and parades to celebrate national holidays and important birthdays. One of the favorite pastimes was kite-flying, and the Chinese were known for their beautiful, colorful kites.

The next dynasty to rule Ancient China was the Zhou Dynasty, which ruled China for nearly 800 years. The Zhou people were warring people who came into power by conquering the Shang. They expanded the territory which the Shang had ruled and divided the land between their relatives. This was not a good plan, and soon, violence broke out between the "states." These groups became known as the Warring States. Each of the warlords had their own army made from the forced armed service of the local peasants and farmers.

Other changes occurred during this time period; iron was used for farming implements and weapons, and cities grew and became stronger. It was also during this time that scholars thought great thoughts about law and order. Perhaps it was the unrest which fed the longing for more peaceful times, for it was during this warring time that the great philosopher, Confucius, proclaimed his philosophies. It would not be until later that his philosophies would be widely popular.

The Zhou Dynasty was followed by the Qin (Chin) Dynasty. Just as the other civilizations had been united by a strong ruler, the Warring States Period was brought to a close by a strong leader. Qin Zheng (chin-ZHUNG), one of the warlords, was mightier than all the others. He easily conquered the others with his million-man army. Qin then united the separate kingdoms and made China bigger and stronger. The name "China" comes from Qin, because Qin Zheng was the first true Emperor of China.

After Qin Zheng became the ruler of China in 221 B.C., he changed his name to Shi Huangdi (SHI-wangdee), which means "first emperor." Qin united China in many ways. He used taxes and laws to make all of his people "equal." He commanded that streets, roads, bridges, and canals be built to better unite his kingdom. He standardized units of weight and measurement, and he started the use of a standard money system. The biggest and most famous project started by Qin was the Great Wall of China. This amazing, nearly three thousand mile wall is the only man-made structure visible from outer space.

Qin had stamped out any rebellion in his kingdom, united the states, and ordered roads and canals to be built, but he still felt unsettled about the northern borders of his kingdom. He knew of the roving tribes of barbarians who had attacked the Warring Tribes. These people would become known as the Mongols, and Qin knew that they could weaken his kingdom if they came into China. There was nothing to keep them from doing this...or was there? Suddenly Qin thought about the walls that the warlords had built around their cities, and he had a brilliant idea! He would command that a wall be built the entire length of his kingdom's northern border.

When Qin told his officers about his idea, they thought he must be crazy; how could anyone build a nearly three thousand mile long wall? There was not enough stone or rock in the entire kingdom for such a wall. Finally, the architects developed a plan; they would use packed-down dirt to construct the wall. It was extremely hard labor, which took a long time, but section by section, the wall was started. Every man in the kingdom was required to work on the wall one month out of the year.

Of course the wall was not finished in Qin's lifetime, but every emperor after him kept the construction going. It took several hundred years, but the Great Wall of China was finally complete. Today, the Great Wall has sections which have tumbled down, but there are many long segments which are still sturdy enough to be walked upon.

After Qin died, a government official, Liu Bang (yoo-BONG), took power and started the Han Dynasty, which lasted four hundred years. This dynasty established new laws and civil service, based on the philosophies of Confucius.

Liu Bang also organized the production of goods, such as silk, iron, and paper, making China a stronger world trader. The Han Dynasty gained control over the eastern end of the silk trade between Europe and Asia. The Han Dynasty emperors also continued the work on the Great Wall, and more canals, bridges, and roads were constructed to unite the country. Houseboats became a common sight on rivers, as thousands of families made them their year-round homes.

The Han Dynasty was followed by the Tang Dynasty. Where the Qin and Han Dynasties developed the industrial and governmental aspects

of the Chinese culture, the Tang Dynasty is known for the development of the fine arts. Music, art, crafts, and literature made monumental advances during the Tang Dynasty, and for three hundred years, China lived in relative peace.

This was also a time of religious experimentation.

Buddhism had spread from India and was now the central religion. Confucianism, which taught a strict code of conduct, was highly endorsed by the government, while Daoism urged simple honesty and "being one with the laws of nature." Each one of these ways of thinking were considered helpful in different areas of life, but just like any other religion, which places value and power anywhere but in God, these beliefs did nothing to help the Chinese people.

To add to the "religion stew," foreigners brought the beliefs of Islam and Christianity (after the beginning of the Christian church). Of course, Christianity, when added to the stew, is not really Christianity. Jesus Christ, our Savior and risen Lord, is the only way to the Father; all other roads do not lead to Heaven or to the heart of God.

Narration Break: discuss the rest of the story. Read "Apologetics through Archaeology" #12.

Ancient African and European Civilizations

Africa, land of deserts and safaris, is the largest "free-standing" continent on Planet Earth. Vast deserts cover enormous areas, and sand, blown by scorching desert winds, form mountainous dunes...

This is the Sahara Desert, land of cacti, lizards, and strange animals, which do not need water often. The only water is found in the oases - lush, little islands of life in middle of the vast stretches.

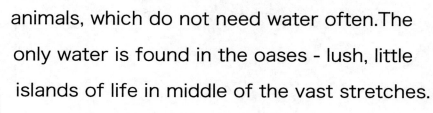

We do not know much about ancient African civilizations because there are very few written records of their way of life. Although there are very few artifacts, fortunately, there are cave paintings.

We can tell by these paintings, the Sahara was not always a desert. There are paintings of farmers sewing and harvesting their crops. There are paintings of children playing in the grass and of mothers dressed in pretty clothes. The people's lives seemed very similar to that of the Egyptians, who lived near the Nile River.

Archaeologists have found remnants of their life, and they have uncovered evidence of the presence of fertile soil, much like

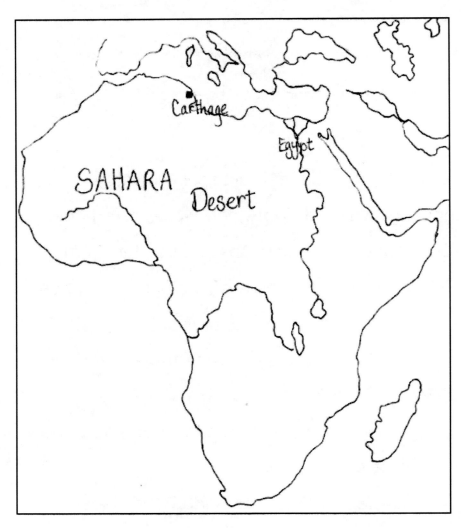

that of the Nile River Valley.

We do not know for sure what happened to this land. We do know that it rained less and less, and the rivers and streams dried up and stopped watering the ground. The land became impossible to farm and unfriendly to human inhabitants. The animals moved further south, where there was more food and water.

The oases that are still there are from the underground springs that did not dry up. Their waters run from underground streams and tributaries and are not affected by the surrounding sand and blistering winds. These oases are a reminder of what this part of Africa used to look like before the desert took over.

The desert would serve as a natural barrier between the people groups of southern and far-northern Africa. No merchants braved the harsh conditions of the desert to travel to the southern part of the continent. In this way, southern Africa was protected from the influence of the other ancient civilizations. Along the northern edge of the continent, however, there were settlers from many civilizations who created their own colonies. To this day, this area of Africa is considered to be part of the Middle East.

Egypt, up in the northeastern corner of Africa, was the prominent civilization, along with two countries, Axum and Nubia, which lie to the south of Egypt. The Bible calls Nubia, Cush (KOOSH), because the descendants of a man, named Cush, settled there. Cush was the eldest son of Ham (the son of Noah) and the father of Nimrod, the man who led the people to build the Tower of Babel. Very early in history, Nubia was conquered and ruled by Egypt for many centuries. Nubians became

more and more like Egyptians in their lifestyles, and like many other conquered peoples, they became like their conquerors. As the land west of Nubia became more and more desert-like, the Nubians decided to stay, because they had the Nile River to water their crops.

Axum was also called Ethiopia. These people grew in wealth and strength through trading with the other merchants of the world. Their main trading port was at Adulis, on the Red Sea. They traded spices and cloth for African elephant tusks, which contained ivory. Ivory was a precious commodity, and they could ask almost any price they wanted. Other merchants were eager to buy the ivory and brought their very best wares to trade. In this way, Ethiopia became a rich country.

Narration Break: discuss the story so far.

To the north of Africa, across the Mediterranean Sea, lies a distinctly boot-shaped peninsula. Today, the country located here is Italy, but in ancient days (1500 - 500 B.C.) the people who lived here were called Celts. The Celts were known for their fine craftsmanship. Artifacts found from these people are quite stunning. Even armor, worn by warriors, was elaborate in design.

Over time, the Celts migrated north into Northern Europe and Britain and south, into what is now Spain. Here they lived and traded with the other merchants, therefore spreading their intricate handiwork throughout the known civilizations. One of the most famous and outstanding Celtic ruins, Stonehenge, is located in southern England. Work on this structure which still standing, started in about 2750 B.C. and took over one thousand years to complete. The workers had to drag enormous rocks to the location, by using a thousand men, pulling an immensely huge sledge. This process took weeks and weeks for each rock because they were taken from a rock quarry which was located

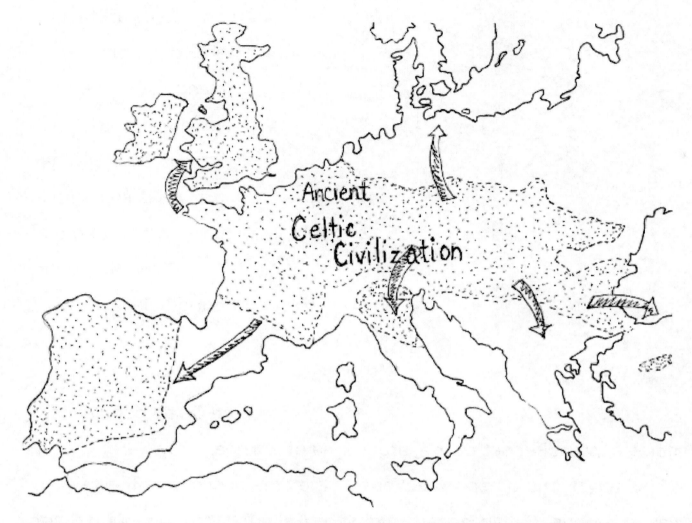

nearly twenty miles away. Like the pyramids of Egypt and the Great Wall of China, Stonehenge was made by human hands and strength alone. There were no cranes or trucks to haul or lift the rocks into place. The builders raised the massive slabs of stone into place by shoving wood under them. The more wood they placed under the rock slab, the higher they hoisted it, until they had it in position to move onto the structure.

Some historians believe this huge, stone, circular structure was used as a calendar, while others think it was used for religious ceremonies.

The Celtic artifacts are found most plentifully in the southern parts of Europe because the ground is so damp in northern Europe that everything that gets buried, decays very quickly.

Around 500 B.C. the Celtic population started spreading out over a larger area of Europe. They were respected by the other civilizations of the time because of their skill in war. A famous Roman leader fought the Celts for the land, but did not win. (We will learn about Julius Caesar and his famous empire in a later chapter.)

The Celts' lifestyle was somewhat nomadic, and they lived in circular wooden huts with thatched roofs. Their clothes were made out of cloth which was woven in intricate tartan designs. The Celts were also quite accomplished at farming. They were well-known for their ingenuity. They invented a reaping machine to help with the harvesting of the grains, and they built massive "hill forts," which were multi-tiered hills, with the village at the very top. This type of fort made it impossible for enemy armies to sneak up on them.

In the early days, the Celts' religious practices were particularly gruesome. I am not going to completely ruin our story by going into the details of their practices, but I will say they practiced witchcraft, and their priests were called Druids. (Eventually, Christianity came to the Celts, and many of them became Christians. In a later volume, we will learn about a very famous "missionary" who ministered to the Celts.) Because the Celts' civilization was so widespread, their influences were felt far and wide. Eventually, the Celts were conquered in southern Europe and were driven to the northern parts again. Even today, you find much Celtic influence in the countries of Ireland and Scotland.

Narration Break: discuss the rest of the story. Read "Apologetics through Archaeology" #13.

Era of the Judges of Israel

This week our winding path through history brings us back to the Children of Israel. When we left their story several weeks ago, they had just entered the Promised Land, the land which God had promised Abraham so many years before. (The time period of their deliverance from Egypt and their wandering in the wilderness is thought to be 1446-1406 or possibly 1290-1250 B.C.) As we know from our studies of the people who lived in Canaan during that time, the land was certainly not empty. The Israelites had to fight for it, but God delivered each city and group of people into their hands when they listened to Him and obeyed.

The Israelites lived in their promised land for many years. They built their own cities and farmed the land. They were very happy to be there, and Joshua, now a very old man, was still considered their honored leader. Joshua lived to be one hundred ten years old, and before he died, he called the people together one last time.

Pause now to read this account of Joshua's last words with the people, in Joshua 23 - 24.

You would think that, after all that God had done for them, the Israelites would be careful to follow God's instructions in every way. But, just like us, they messed up. After Joshua's death, they turned their backs on God, an they worshipped idols of the Canaanites. They also married Canaanite women, which angered God, and he allowed them to be conquered and ruled by the king of Mesopotamia. The Israelites lived under the reign of this king for eight long years. Oh, how they wished they had listened and obeyed God! They finally turned back to God and cried out for help.

God sent them a warrior named Othniel (OTH-nee-el), who was the nephew of Caleb. It was Caleb who had stood with Joshua in believing that God could deliver the city of Jericho into their hands, and now it was Othniel who stood up to fight the king of Mesopotamia. God used this brave man to defeat the enemy and, once again, free His people. Othniel ruled Israel as a judge for forty years, and during this time, there was peace and prosperity in Israel.

After Othniel was dead, Israel once again drifted into rebellion. They wanted to be like their neighbors, who all had gods that could be seen and touched. Never mind that these gods were created by human hands out of wood, ivory, or rock. Never mind that they were powerless to help or that they were worthless pieces of junk; no, the Israelites were not satisfied with their God, Who had delivered them from the hand of the most powerful king on the face of the earth. They had a very short attention span and an even shorter memory of the trouble which they got into every time they turned their backs on God.

Again, God allowed foreign kings to attack and conquer Israel. This time, it was the king of Moab who attacked, and with the help of other enemies of Israel, he became the new ruler of Israel. God had withdrawn His hand of protection from His people, but He was still there. He still watched over them and waited for them to repent. For eighteen long years, the Israelites were oppressed by the Moabites, and again, they grew weary of being without the protection of God. They decided to return to Him and beg for His forgiveness.

It completely amazes me how patient our God is! He is so loving and kind even when we do not deserve it. Once again, He sent someone to deliver the Israelites from the hands of their enemies. This time, the chosen leader's name was Ehud. After they had broken free from the Moabites, they lived in peace. Judges 3:30 says that the Israelites had rest for eighty years.

The next judge to rule Israel was Shamgar (SHAM-gar), who helped defeat the Philistines. Shamgar was followed by a mighty woman of God named Deborah. Israel was once again slipping into their familiar rebellion and disobedience, when Deborah took a stand. She had the gift of prophecy, and God told her many things that would happen if the Israelites did not obey. Deborah led the people of Israel against the cruel oppressors who were making life miserable for the Israelites. Deborah and a man of God, named Barak, who was a brave soldier, led the people in obedience to God. They were considered judges of Israel

and honored by all of the people.
For forty years, Deborah and
Barak lead the Children of Israel,
and there was peace in the land
again.

Of course, as you might
suspect by now, the Israelites
wandered away from God again
after Deborah and Barak were
gone. They returned to their idols
and worshipped worthless gods
again. This time, there was a
group of people called the Midianites, who were eyeing the land of
Israel. God withdrew His hand of protection from His wayward,
disobedient children and allowed the Midianites to move in on them.
They literally moved into the land, and like a swarm of grasshoppers,
they ate up and consumed everything the Israelites had. Their crops
and homes were destroyed by these pesky neighbors. When they had
been overrun with the Midianites, once again, the Children of Israel
came to their senses and cried out to the Lord for help.

As usual, God had a special person chosen to help His people.
Gideon was not from a rich family. He was not the oldest of his
brothers. He did not have the strength to drive out the swarms of

pesky, parasitic people, who were plaguing his people! What Gideon did have, though, was a powerful God, in Whom he believed and trusted. God knew He could trust Gideon to carry out His orders, and He delivered the Israelites from the Midianites.

Gideon was judge for forty years, and he was followed by Tola, Jair, Jephthah, Ibzan, Elon, Abdon, Samson, Eli, and Samuel. This last judge of Israel, Samuel, was a highly respected man of God, and we will learn more about him in our next chapter. Throughout all of these judges, Israel drifted back and forth between obedience and rebellion.

◯ Optional (but highly suggested for at least adults and older children) Bible reading: the book of Judges; this might be a good time to read from a trusted Bible story book, such as Egermeier's.

Narration Break: discuss the story so far.

During the time of the judges, there was a godly, Hebrew man named Elimelech (e-LIM-u-lec), who lived in the land of Judah with his wife, Naomi (na-O-me), and his two small sons. There came to Judah a harsh famine, so Elimelech moved his family to the nearby land of

Moab. This land had plenty of food, but life here was a difficult adjustment for them. Their Moabite neighbors all worshipped false gods and had never heard of the One true God. Elimelech and Naomi stood firm in their faith in God, and they taught their sons to worship Him, too. Then the family suffered a terrible shock; Elimelech died. Now Naomi had no one but her sons.

Naomi's sons, Mahlon (MAY-lon) and Chilion (CHIL-ee-on), took care of their mother until they were grown. When they were old enough, they both married young ladies from Moab, Ruth and Orpah. Ruth became a follower of God also, and she loved her mother-in-law very much. Their happiness was not to last long, however, for once again, tragedy struck the family. Both Mahlon and Chilion died, leaving Naomi, Ruth, and Orpah alone and without protection.

Word reached Naomi that the famine was over in Judah, and so she decided to return to her homeland. Both of her daughters-in-law wanted to travel back with her, and she agreed to let them come part of the way. When they had traveled a short distance, Naomi told them to return to their families and remarry. Orpah kissed her mother-in-law goodbye and returned to the land of

But Ruth replied, "Don't urge me to leave you or to turn back from you. Where you go I will go, and where you stay I will stay. Your people will be my people and your God my God. 17 Where you die I will die, and there I will be buried. May the Lord deal with me, be it ever so severely, if even death separates you and me."

Moab, but Ruth absolutely refused. She hugged Naomi close and declared resolutely, "Do not try to make me leave you! I will go wherever you go. I will live where you live. Your people will be my people, and your God will be my God!" Naomi knew Ruth wanted to stay with her and take care of her, and with lighter steps, the two women continued their journey to Bethlehem.

When the women reached their destination, Naomi's friends were overjoyed to see her. They were shocked, however, at the change they saw in their friend's face; the grief and sorrow she had suffered had etched deep lines on her once-smooth face. Naomi told her gathered friends to call her Mara, which means "bitter and sorrowful," because God had taken away everything she once had. She no longer wanted her name to be Naomi, which means "pleasant."

It was harvest time in Israel at the time of Naomi's return. The fields were full of ripe grain and the harvesters were reaping. In Ancient Israel, there was a custom which helped the poor among them. As the reapers went through binding up the bundles of grain, they left some of the harvest for the the poor to gather. When Ruth heard about this practice, she begged Naomi to allow her to gather this grain.

Naomi knew the field, in which Ruth wanted to glean, belonged to one of her rich relatives. This relative was a godly man named Boaz (BO-az), and he was considered to be her husband's close kin. When Boaz saw Ruth gleaning in his field, he asked his workmen who she was, and

when they answered that
she was a Moabite who
had returned with her
mother-in-law, Naomi, Boaz
commanded them to leave
plenty of grain for her to
glean. He then told Ruth to
not glean at any other field
and to refresh herself
from his maidservants'
water jars.

Boaz watched as Ruth
worked diligently to gather
food for Naomi and
herself. She did not flirt with the workers, and she was modest and
quiet. Boaz admired her and decided to ask for permission to marry her.
There was one other relative who was closer than he. Boaz went to this
man and asked him if Boaz could take his place as the "kinsman
redeemer." A kinsman redeemer is a male relative who marries a widow
and redeems the family line, by giving her a child to carry on the name.
He also buys the family's land, which is being forfeited, therefore
redeeming the family fortune as well as the legacy. Boaz acquired
permission to marry Ruth and to take care of Naomi.

Ruth married Boaz, and together, they had a little boy. This little boy was named Obed (O-bed). Obed grew up to have a son named Jesse, and Jesse became the father of David. Ruth, the Moabite woman, who came to believe in the One true God, became the Grandmother of the great King David and the matron of the lineage of Jesus, our Savior.

☺ Optional (but highly suggested for at least adults and older children) Bible reading: the book of Ruth; this might be a good time to read from a trusted Bible story book such as Egermeier's.

Narration Break: discuss the story of Ruth.

This story thrills me to my fingertips, and I am chuckling as I write it because God amazes me with His absolutely perfect plans. He had promised Abraham that He would make his family a great nation, a nation from which He would bring the Messiah. God can redeem every situation, every sorrowful soul, every broken heart. He sent Boaz to be Ruth's kinsman redeemer, and He used him to be a symbol of what Jesus would be for all of us. REDEEMER! Before we finish this section of our story, I want to let you in on a little background information about Boaz.

Turn to Matthew 1: 1-6. Do you see who the mother of Boaz is? Rahab! Do you remember when you read the Scriptures about how Moses sent spies into Canaan to look around? Do you remember the woman (prostitute), Rahab, in Jericho? Do you see how God used Boaz's marriage to Ruth as a redemption of his own family line? The God of the Universe, the Ancient of Days knows all of our stories - He is in the process of weaving an intricately beautiful tapestry which we call history.

The Great Kings of Israel

The last judge of Israel was named Samuel, and his story is one worth reading. Before continuing with our story in this chapter, take time to read the following Bible passage.

I Samuel 1 - 2 (The story of the beginning of Samuel's life)

In our last chapter, we learned the Israelites turned their backs on God time and again. I cannot help but think that they really were not so very different from us; we tend to turn to God more in times of trouble, than in times of peace. Sometimes, just like with the Israelites, hard times come to us so we will turn to Him. What a comfort it should be to all of us that He is always there. He is our Redeemer and King.

Speaking of kings... up to this time, Israel had not had a king. In fact, God had specifically told them that they did not need a king because they had Him to lead them. As usual, they did not listen; they demanded to have a king like their neighbors. Samuel, who grew up to replace Eli as the judge of Israel, tried to counsel the Children of Israel to listen to God. He begged them to trust Him, because He knew what was best for them. They did not listen and demanded that Samuel find them a king. With a sigh, Samuel asked God to give the Israelites a king.

God gave them a king from the tribe of Benjamin. He told Samuel that a young man, named Saul, would come looking for some lost donkeys. The Lord told Samuel to anoint the young man as King of Israel. Saul was amazed that he had been chosen to be the first king of

Israel. After all, he was from a small family, of the smallest tribe, of Israel.

For a time, Saul obeyed what God said to do. Samuel worked closely with him to help him make wise decisions, but after a while, Saul became more accustomed to being king. He became arrogant and did not obey what Samuel told him were God's directions. Samuel was sad, because he knew Saul's heart was becoming full of pride and selfish ambition. He told Saul God was already looking for a man who would obey Him to become the next king. Saul had forfeited his family's kingly line because of his disobedience.

Saul had a son, named Jonathan, who was a heroic soldier and a godly man. Over the years, Saul became more and more protective of his position as king. He wanted to make sure Jonathan would take his place on the throne when he died. Even though Saul knew Samuel had said that his family would not carry on the line of kings, Saul was determined to make it so. Samuel watched this king, whom he had anointed as a young man. His heart ached, because he knew God had removed His favor from him, and as long as Saul was king, He would not bless Israel. Samuel mourned for Saul as though he had died.

> "Does the Lord delight in burnt offerings and sacrifices as much as in obeying the Lord? To obey is better than sacrifice, and to heed is better than the fat of rams."
>
> 1 Samuel 15:22

God came to Samuel and told him to stop mourning and weeping for Saul. God told the old prophet He had chosen another man to become king. This was a man after God's own heart. Can you imagine being described, in the Bible, as the man (or woman) after God's own heart? Isn't that simply thrilling? This chosen one was the son of Jesse. You will remember we learned in our last chapter about the woman, named Ruth, who had a son named Obed. This Obed grew up to have a son named Jesse, and Jesse became the father of eight sons, of which the youngest was David.

Poor, old Samuel! By this time, he must have felt like he had created a monster. Saul had turned into an arrogant, self-serving, depressed, and angry individual, and no doubt, Samuel was a bit afraid of him. In

1 Samuel 16:2, it says Samuel asked God how he could go anoint another king, because Saul would kill him if he found out. God helped Samuel by telling him to take a young heifer (female cow) for a sacrifice and to go to the town of Bethlehem, where David's family lived.

When Samuel met each of Jesse's sons, he thought that this one must be the chosen one, for each seemed to be bigger, stronger, and better looking than the last. But God told Samuel that He looks at the heart, while men look on the outside. Finally, David, the last and youngest, was called in from the fields where he was watching his father's sheep. As the young man stood in front of Samuel, God said, "This is the one. This is the one after My own heart. Anoint him as king."

At the time of his anointing, David was a very young man. The Bible says he was ruddy (which means of the red-haired complexion) and handsome to look at. Can you just imagine what was running through David's mind as he knelt before Samuel? Just a few minutes before, he was the lowliest of his brothers, a shepherd who spent many hours out in the pasturelands with his fathers sheep, playing his harp and singing to the Lord. Now, here he was, kneeling before Samuel, the famous prophet, hearing the words of the blessing and feeling the oil dribbling down his neck. King? How could he be king?

You would think after being anointed king, David would have gone and taken the throne. This did not happen, though. Instead, David returned to his father's sheep, and Saul remained on the throne.

Nothing looked like it had changed at all. In fact, as the weeks slipped by, I am sure David might have felt the whole anointing was a dream, but God had been planning this for a long time. He had it all worked out.

King Saul's mental health was very fragile by this time. He was paranoid about everything, and the Bible says God allowed an evil spirit to torment him.

He became so depressed, it was suggested that someone, was skilled at playing the harp, should come and sooth his jangled nerves with music. It was known that Jesse of Bethlehem happened to have a son who was a skilled harpist. And so it was that David was brought to the palace to play the harp for King Saul. The harp music soothed the troubled soul and spirit of the king.

🌑 1 Samuel 13 (Saul's first disobedience to the laws of God)

🌑 1 Samuel 16:1-13 (Samuel anoints David)

Chapter 15

Narration Break: discuss the story so far. After reading the assigned reading above, discuss how Saul become arrogant and self-serving.

The Bible says Saul loved David. Saul's son, Jonathan, and David became the very best of friends, and from very early on, Jonathan knew David was chosen by God to be the next king of Israel. Instead of being jealous of David, Jonathan made a covenant with him to be loyal and protect him. When Saul began to feel better, David returned to his home and continued caring for his father's sheep.

It was around this time, the Philistines rose up against the Israelites again. The armies camped facing each other, as was the custom back in that time. Everyday, the Philistines would taunt the Israelites and call them names. One day they challenged the Israelites to send out their mightiest warrior to fight their own mightiest warrior. The Israelites were tired of all the insults, so they accepted the challenge. When they saw the Philistines' prized warrior, they shook in their armor! There before them, stood the biggest human being they had ever seen. This giant, Goliath, stood before them and hurled insults and slurs against them and their God. Day after day, the Israelites hid from him, as he sent his challenge to come fight.

David's brothers were in the Israelite army and had been away from home long enough to worry Jesse, so he sent young David to bring them food and provisions. When David rode into the camp, he heard the bellowing of the belligerent, barbarous brute, Goliath. He wondered why the Israelite army was hiding. They had God on their side; why should they be afraid of this oaf? David went straight to King Saul's tent and told him he would fight this Philistine giant. At first, Saul thought David was crazy and refused to let him go, but David insisted that God had helped him kill a lion and a bear while he had been watching his father's sheep. If God could deliver these wild animals into his hands, then this Philistine brute would be no different.

Finally, Saul relented and said that David could go, but he would have to wear Saul's armor. After trying the armor on and not being able to move, David decided to go out with his own clothes, his trusty slingshot, and most importantly, faith in his God. David walked out to the creek to find the perfect stones for his slingshot.

David must not have made a very impressive sight, standing there in his shepherd's clothes with his slingshot at his side. The Bible says David ran at Goliath. He didn't tippy-toe, he didn't drag his feet, he ran at the enemy. The very sight of him angered Goliath to the point of screaming; he hurled insults against David, the Israelites, and God. David calmly placed a stone in his slingshot, and with God guiding his arm, slung it straight and true. Deep into Goliath's forehead went the stone, and down came the giant. David used Goliath's own sword to finish the job, and the petrified Philistines ran away in terror.

David was an instant hero throughout Israel, which made Saul jealous. Over the next few years, King Saul's jealousy toward David escalated. Eventually, David had to run for his life and live in hiding for years. Even though he knew God had chosen him to be the next king, he also knew he had to wait for Him to show him the right time. When many years had passed, Saul and Jonathan both died in a battle, and God moved David out from hiding and into his position as King.

One of my favorite books in the Bible is Psalms. This wonderful book was written by several authors, and one of them is King David. Even though he was a man after God's own heart, he was very human. He fell and had to ask for forgiveness. He overstepped the bounds of his authority and was disciplined by God, but he always turned back to God and asked for forgiveness. David was truly the greatest king of Israel and a wonderful example for us today. I would like very much for all of the readers of this story to become acquainted with David. His story is in First and Second Samuel, and his songs and prayers are recorded in Psalms.

During David's reign, the nation of Israel became a "super-power" of that time period. With God's help, he conquered the enemies of Israel, laying to waste the nations who had caused so much trouble during Saul's reign. David was quite the paradox; he was a warrior, poet, musician, and great politician. He certainly had God's blessing on his life. David loved God with all of his heart, and he wanted to build God a permanent temple. As you learned in your assigned Bible readings, the Israelites had built a tabernacle according to God's direction while they were in the wilderness (Exodus 25 - 29). David wanted God to have a beautiful and elaborate temple, but God told him that he was not the king who would build it. David's son, Solomon, was to be the one to build this special house for God.

Solomon was the third king of Israel. Even though David had other sons, God had chosen Solomon to be King after David died. David had reigned over Israel for forty years, and his people loved him. When Solomon became king, he knew he needed God to help him to be a good, godly king, as his father had been. He burned an offering of a thousand animals, and while they burned upon the altar, Solomon prayed to God for the help he knew he needed.

God saw Solomon's heart, and it made Him happy to see that the new king had a humble heart. God came to Solomon in a dream and asked him what he wanted most. Solomon knew how much he would need an understanding heart to be a good king, so this is what he asked for. This pleased God so much, he not only gave Solomon wisdom as he asked for, but He also gave the new king riches and power.

Solomon became known as such a wise king that people from far away came to ask him for help in settling disputes. God also gave Solomon wisdom to know how to build the great temple that David had wanted to build. Cedar trees from Lebanon were cut down to be used for the temple, along with huge slabs of marble and granite. He hired Phoenician artisans and builders to help.

During Solomon's reign, God made the Children of Israel into a mighty nation. For many years, Solomon obeyed God and did what was right, but as he got older, he started to slowly slide in the wrong direction. Perhaps he forgot it was God who had given him his wisdom and wealth. He married women from other nations and, to make them happy, he made them temples for their gods. This made God angry, and He told Solomon his kingdom would be given to a servant named Jeroboam (j[air]-u-BO-um).

As His chosen people, Israel was God's focus during this time period. Just as He does now, He knew what was going on everywhere all over the world, but Israel was the apple of His eye. He knew that from Israel would come the Messiah - the Savior of all mankind. The other civilizations, which were simultaneously occupying the earth at the time, offered a colorful backdrop. This does not mean the other people of the earth were not important to God, though. After all, He was planning a Messiah for the entire world.

⬤1 Kings 3 - 4 (God's gift to Solomon)

Narration Break: discuss the story of David and Solomon. Read "Apologetics through Archaeology" #14 & 15.

Over the next several weeks, your special assignment is to read certain parts of the story of David. There is so much written about him and his sons that it is important to read at least some of it. Divide the readings in manageable sections.

1 Sam. 17:1-54 (David and Goliath) 1 Sam.19-27 (accounts of David fleeing Saul) 2 Sam. 2:4-6:18 (David becomes king) 2 Sam. 11:1-12:25 (David's sin with Bathsheba)

Ancient Greece

In an earlier chapter, we learned about an ancient civilization called the Mycenaeans. These people were considered to be the earliest people of Greece, and they ruled their peninsula for hundreds of years. Not only did they rule the mainland of Greece, but they had taken over a large island country that lies to the south. The island country, Crete, had, at one time, been a peaceful farming civilization. The people, who lived there, had lived in peace for centuries, because their small island country was completely surrounded by the vast Mediterranean Sea, which protected them from invasion. These people became known for their skill in ship-building. They were also known for a rather strange "sport," bull jumping!

Bull jumping was the Cretans' favorite form of entertainment. Young children were trained from a very young age to perform in this dangerous "sport." As the bull came raging into the ring, the bull jumpers grabbed its horns and somersaulted onto its back, flipping up and over the beast, landing in the ring behind them.

The people who lived on Crete were called Minoans, after a famous, legendary king - King Minos. The Minoans lived on Crete for a long time, and then something mysterious happened; they all moved away in a short period of time. Historians believe that a volcano erupted on the island of Thera, which was not far from Crete. The volcanic ash was washed over the sea to Crete, destroying farmland and towns. After the volcano erupted, and the Minoans were mostly gone, the Mycenaeans came and took over Crete.

The Mycenaeans thought they were highly civilized and superior compared to other people around them. They were skilled warriors and weapon-makers. They knew how to make their weapons out of iron and other metals, they knew how to read and write, and they thought they could not be conquered by the roaming nomadic "herds" of people, who lived to the north of them. These northern people were called "barbarians" because they were thought to be uncouth and ignorant. What they did know how to do was fight and make iron weapons.

The time period, which followed between the years 1100 and 700 B.C. are known as the Dark Ages in Greece because so very little is known about them. It is known that some new people, called the Dorians, came into Greece and invaded the Mycenaeans. Many aspects of their culture changed. There were no more palaces built for the rulers, and everyone lived more simply. Even the method of burying their dead changed. In earlier years, the Mycenaeans had held elaborate ceremonies and buried their dead in intricate tombs, along with their favorite riches; now, they cremated their dead. As the Dorians overtook their country, the Mycenaeans' culture changed as well. Their country was divided up into separate city-states, including Corinth, Athens, and Sparta. These city-states fought amongst themselves quite frequently.

Although there is not much known as fact about this time period, there are many myths and legends, which have been passed down for centuries. It was during this time, though historians disagree exactly when, that a famous poet lived. (In truth, the very existence of this Ancient Greek poet is debated by many.) Homer, the blind poet, who was thought to live sometime between 850 and 1200 B.C., is attributed with writing the epic poems "The Iliad" and "The Odyssey." These poems are thought to tell great and heroic tales of a war that rocked Greece during ancient days. "The Iliad" is the first poem and tells the tale of Odysseus (o-DIS-ee-us), a gallant warrior who fought in the war, and "The Odyssey" is the second part of the tale.

The Trojan War is one of the most important events in Greek mythology. Historians have argued for years about the authenticity of this war, though writings have been found, on Hittite artifacts, mentioning a Greek war that would have been set during the 1200's B.C. After the narration break, you will read a story that has gone down in history as a possible event during the Trojan War.

Narration Break: discuss the story so far.

The Trojan Horse

Once upon a time, many centuries ago, there was an ancient city named Troy. This city was situated on the coast of Asia, across the Aegean Sea from the Greek city-state, Sparta.

In those days, people built walls around their cities to help protect them. Some walls were only a few feet high, while others were twenty feet high.

These protective walls had gates that could be opened to let people into the city. In times of war, though, the gates were closed and locked to stop the invaders from getting inside the city.

All along the inside of the wall, a winding set of stairs climbed to the top. Soldiers stood at the top of the stairs and shot arrows down at the enemy who was trying to get inside the city. There were also special holes built high on the wall, through which archers shot arrows as well. Most of the time, these walls were quite effective in keeping the attacking armies on the outside of the city. If the wall was breached, the city would be under siege, and an enemy conquest was almost assured.

The walls around the city of Troy were exceptionally strong and tall. According to this legend, the Greeks had been trying to breach the wall around Troy for ten long years. The Greeks could not get over the wall, and the Trojans could not drive the Greeks away. Year after year they fought, and year after year, neither side won.

One day, Odysseus, a Greek general, had an idea. "Let us trick our enemy by pretending to sail away," he suggested. "We will leave a gift for Troy to announce the end of the war. It will be a wooden horse with thirty men hidden inside. At night, these men can sneak out and open the gate of Troy!" This was the custom for admitting defeat in those days; you offered a gift to the victorious army. It could be a gift of money, art, slaves, or a huge horse sculpture. The Greeks were famous for their art, so the horse would be easy to design and construct.

The Greeks thought it was a brilliant idea. They had their best artists build the magnificent horse. When it was ready, the Greeks brought the enormous, wooden horse as close to Troy's city gates as they could get without being shot full of arrows; then they pretended to sail away.

When the Trojan archers at the top of the stairs saw the Greeks leaving, they could not believe their eyes. Were the Greeks giving up at last? Had the Trojans won the war? It certainly appeared so! They dragged the horse inside their city and closed the gates. They celebrated their victory!

Some of people wanted to burn the horse, which would have been a sad fate for the Greek soldiers hidden inside, but the others said, "No, it is too beautiful! We will keep it as a reminder of our victory!" The Greeks had counted on the Trojans reacting this way because the Trojans were famous for their bragging. The Greeks knew the Trojans would want to display their magnificent horse, and they were right!

That night, after the Trojans slept soundly, exhausted from their celebrations, the thirty Greek soldiers hiding inside the wooden horse, climbed out and opened the gates of Troy to let the Greek army inside. That was the end of Troy!

So why in the world would we want to learn about a legend such as the Trojan Horse? What is the big deal? When we are talking about history during this ancient time period, we are not always sure where the line between fact and fiction is located. In fact, there are so many conflicting accounts, of almost every happening in history, that it would be impossible to include only those accounts which were 100%

absolutely true. We do know that this ancient account of the Trojan War has been found in several different ancient writings.
This is how it is mentioned in Homer's "Odyssey"...

"What a thing was this, to which that mighty man wrought and endured in the carven horse, wherein all we chiefs of the Argives were sitting, bearing to the Trojans death and fate! But come now, change their theme, and sing of the building of the horse of wood, which Epeius made with Athena's help the horse which once Odysseus led up into the citadel as a thing of guile, when he had filled it with the men who sacked lion.

This is the most detailed, most familiar account. This is from a literary work by Virgil, a Roman poet.

After many years have slipped by, the leaders of the Greeks,

opposed by the Fates, and damaged by the war,

build a horse of mountainous size, through Pallas's divine art,

and weave planks of fir over its ribs:

they pretend it's a votive offering: this rumor spreads.

They secretly hide a picked body of men, chosen by lot,

there, in the dark body, filling the belly and the huge

cavernous insides with armed warriors.

....

Then Laocoön rushes down eagerly from the heights

of the citadel, to confront them all, a large crowd with him,

and shouts from far off: 'O unhappy citizens, what madness?

Do you think the enemy's sailed away? Or do you think

any Greek gift's free of treachery? Is that Ulysses's reputation?

Either there are Greeks in hiding, concealed by the wood,

or it's been built as a machine to use against our walls,

or spy on our homes, or fall on the city from above,

or it hides some other trick: Trojans, don't trust this horse.

Whatever it is, I'm afraid of Greeks even those bearing gifts.'

Narration Break: discuss the rest of the story. Read "Apologetics through Archaeology" #16.

A Kingdom Divided

Before I started writing this chapter of our story, I took a meandering stroll, back through our story, up to this point. We have seen God show His mighty power through a global flood, which wiped away all evil of that day. We saw Him deliver His chosen people from slavery and bring a shepherd boy to the throne of Israel. This whole story of amazing patience, with the human race, has hit me afresh. God is simply astounding. He is so far above us, and His thoughts are so much higher than ours, that it brings me to my knees. How could the God of the universe, the Maker of all things, the Ancient of Days love us? We are so imperfect. Even when we try with all of our might to be good like Him, our "good" is like muck compared to Him, yet He loves us anyway.

As I have written this story, as the elements and characters have woven themselves into the colorful tapestry, which we call Ancient History, my heart beats faster. With every chapter we walk through together, we move closer to the climax of all history. My heart beats faster, because I know the pattern of humanity's helplessness and hopelessness is about to be broken forever. We are getting closer to the Messiah! We have met the people who God chose to be the earthly lineage of His biggest plan - the plan of redemption. We have watched Ruth glean the fields of a kind, godly man, who would become her kinsman redeemer. And through their union in marriage, the line to King David was put into motion.

King David - a man after God's own heart - the king who led Israel mightily for forty years, is an incredible example of how God looks at the heart. David was not perfect. In fact, he stumbled and fell into horrible sin, but he reached out his trembling, human hand to grasp the hand of his forgiving, Heavenly Father. Through the stories of David, we see and are assured that God does not hold our human-ness against us. If our hearts cry out, "I want to be like You. I want my heart to be like Yours. Align my heart to Yours," He answers our prayers.

After David's son, Solomon, died around the year 930 B.C., the tribes of Israel were divided into two kingdoms. The Northern Kingdom, which was ruled by Jeroboam, just as God had said, kept the name "Israel." The Southern Kingdom, which was called "Judah," was made up mostly of the tribes of Judah and Benjamin. These two tribes were ruled by Solomon's son, Rehoboam (ray-hu-BO-um). Please note, what we discussed in our last chapter was happening around this same time when Israel was divided and ruled by a procession of kings.

These kings ruled the kingdoms for the next three hundred years. Some of these kings were good and God-fearing, while others were not. lAlso during this time, there were prophets among God's people. The godly kings trusted these prophets to give sound advice concerning the rule of the people, but during the reigns of the evil kings, the prophets had to hide or run for their lives.

We will not look at all of these kings and prophets, but we will study a few of the most important. To begin with, Jeroboam, ruler of the Northern Kingdom (Israel), was not a good man. He knew God had moved him, from the place of being a servant to the throne, but he did not want to serve or trust Him. Instead, he worshipped idols and encouraged his people to worship them also. He made God very angry. God spoke through the prophet Ahijah (u-HI-ju) to King Jeroboam and said that, because the king had disobeyed Him, his son would die. This prophecy did come true, and the child died.

Rehoboam, the son of Solomon and a heathen princess, also worshipped idols. Rehoboam was followed by his son, Abijah (u-BI-ju), who ruled for only three years. Asa, son of Abijah, was the next king. Unlike his father and grandfather, Asa feared and followed God. He removed the idols they had set up in the temples of the Lord, and he told his people to follow God. Asa also set about fortifying the walls of Jerusalem. God prospered Judah during Asa's reign, and he gave Judah strength to conquer their enemies from Ethiopia. When the king of Israel saw the success of Judah, he became jealous. Soon there was fighting between the two kingdoms. In our next section, we will learn more about the prophets of this time. Please take the time to read more about these kings.

☻ 1 Kings 12 - 13 (The account of how the kingdom of Israel was  divided) (Chapters 14 and 15 are more information about this time period and the idol worship in both kingdoms.)

☻ 1 Kings 15, 2 Chronicles 12 -15 (The account of Asa's reign)

☻ This may be a good time to read, from the Bible or Egermeier's the accounts of the kings of Israel and Judah during this time period.

Narration Break: discuss the story so far.

During these years of the kings, who ruled the divided kingdom of Israel, there were great prophets of the Lord. One of these godly men was Elijah. He was faithful to remind the people to worship and follow God. Sometimes they listened, but sometimes they did not. Sometimes the kings would listen and obey, but sometimes they hated hearing the truth and persecuted Elijah, instead. Sometimes Elijah had to run for his life because the king wanted to kill him for what he was preaching.
I love the story of this faithful man!

☻ The story of Elijah is in I Kings 16, 17, 18, 19, and 2 Kings 2. Over the next several days, read these chapters and/or the account of  Elijah in Egermeier's Bible Story Book (or a Bible story book of your choice).

Elijah was followed by a young man named Elisha. Like his teacher, Elijah, Elisha was a godly man who did his best to lead the people of Israel in the ways of the Lord. God used him in mighty ways, and Elisha is known as one of the greatest prophets in the history of Israel.

This time period of kings and prophets is a very interesting era in the history of the world. There are so many names, however, that it can be very confusing. Please study the outline of this time period; it covers the next two pages. Also complete the Bible reading assignments listed at the end of the chapter. There are special Student Journal pages to help with learning the important facts from this chapter.

After studying the outline on the previous two pages, please read these accounts in the Bible (for adults and older children) or in the Egermeier's Bible Story Book (for younger children and/or those who need an abbreviated version).

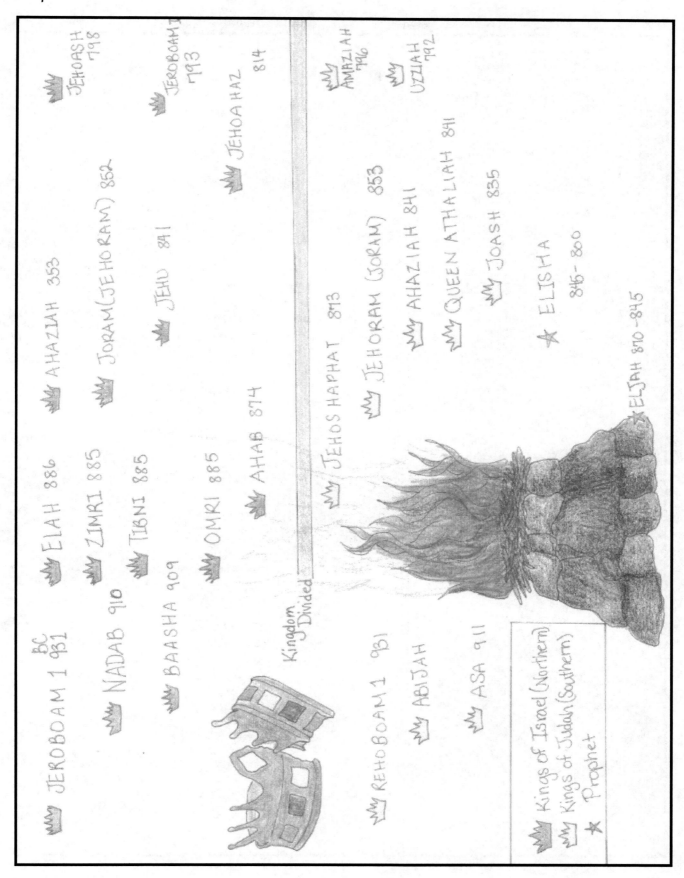

ZECHARIAH 753

SHALLUM 752

PEKAHIAH 742

HOSEA 732

MENAHEM 752

PEKAH 752

ISRAEL FALLS 722
Assyrians Defeat Israel

NAHUM 658-615

JEREMIAH 650-582

ZEPHANIAH 640-626

EZEKIEL 620-570

HABAKKUK 608-598

HEZEKIAH 716
Showed the Babylonian representative the Temple treasures

AHAZ (JEHOAHAZ) 735

JOTHAM 750

ISAIAH 760-673

MICAH 738-698

Jonah 781

AMOS 765-784

HOSEA 758-785

First Exile 605
(Daniel & his friends captured)

AMON 643

JOSIAH 641

MANASSEH 697

JEHOAHAZ 609

JEHOIAKIM 609

DANIEL 620-540

Chapter 17

🌚 The rest of 2 Kings and both 1 and 2 Chronicles gives a detailed account of what was happening at this time.

🌚 The books of Amos, Micah, Nahum, Habakkuk, and Zephaniah tell about the other prophets.

Narration Break: discuss this time period in Israel.

Please take the time to read these accounts in the Bible or a trusted Bible story book.

"Oh King, We Will Not Bow!"

This is the story of one of my absolute favorite people in the Bible. In our last chapter, we read about the divided kingdom of Israel and the kings who ruled them. One of those kings of Judah, named Hezekiah, who was given a special gift from God. It seems Hezekiah was sick unto death, and he cried out to God for help. He begged God to give him fifteen more years to live, and he was granted this request.

While he was sick, however, Hezekiah had visitors, from other nations, who came to wish him well. One of these visitors was from the great city of Babylon, which, by this time, had grown supremely powerful. This Babylonian visitor was apparently an ambassador of good wishes for the ailing king of Judah. King Hezekiah was so flattered by the attention, he showed his Babylonian visitor the treasures of Judah. The golden goblets, rare gems, and precious items that were meant to be set apart for use in the house of God were displayed before him.

When a prophet of God chastised King Hezekiah and told him Babylon would come to plunder and conquer Judah in coming generations, the king was complacent. He was not concerned because at least there would be peace in his lifetime. The Babylonian visitor took a detailed account of the treasures of Judah back to Babylon. This account which was passed from generation to generation for the next one hundred years.

The Book of Daniel begins in the summer of 605 B.C. We have been introduced to the great and mighty Babylon earlier in our story, but as the curtain rises on this act of our drama, it is on the very pinnacle of Babylonian power.

Babylon... the name is scattered like grass seed throughout scripture. She is a symbol of all things evil and self-serving, and in a spiritual sense, she is still alive and strong today. The natural city of Babylon, which was destroyed many hundreds of years ago, is painted vividly in the Book of Daniel, and again, in Revelations. The Babylon of 605 B.C. was a fortress of incredible beauty and strength. Her wall was 56 miles long, and inside its seemingly impenetrable protection, were over two hundred square miles of fabulous dwellings of many kinds. There were numerous, exotic temples to various gods, and let us not overlook the towering 650 foot tall ziggurat, glimmering as the sun reflects off of its enamel sides. This tower is hauntingly similar to the Tower of Babel; both towers stand as the symbol of human rebellion against God. The people of Babylon lived for one reason, and that was self-gratification. They were number one in every way: power, affluence, and riches.

This is the Babylon that Daniel and his friends were thrust into. These were the young men of Judah, the hope of the future. These were not just some boys, who the Babylonian invaders stumbled across and decided to enslave. These young men were special. They were the cream of the crop, the leaders of their generation. They came from well-off families and even the nobility, and they were versed in the ways of

the God of Israel. They knew the history of their people, and they understood they were set apart for the work of the Lord.

The Book of Daniel starts like this...

"In the third year of the reign of Jehoiakim king of Judah came Nebuchadnezzar king of Babylon unto Jerusalem, and besieged it. ²And the Lord gave Jehoiakim king of Judah into his hand, with part of the vessels of the house of God: which he carried into the land of Shinar to the house of his god; and he brought the vessels into the treasure house of his god."

Not only did the heathen King Nebuchadnezzar (neb-u-cad-NEZ-zar) take the prized young men as his plunder, he also took the vessels of the house of God. Think about this for a moment. Since the Israelites had left Egypt, these vessels had been set apart for the sacred service of God. Wow. I don't know about you, but this gives me the shivers. I do not think King Nebuchadnezzar realized the ramifications of what he had done.

The Bible does not tell us exactly how many young men of Judah were taken into captivity, but there were a great number of them. It is interesting to read in the Book of Daniel that they were to be given the very best from the table of the Babylonian king. Do not think that Nebuchadnezzar was being kind to them. He knew the Israelites had strict dietary laws, and this order to eat the foods from his table was actually a way to defile them. This is when we meet Daniel and his two friends for the first time.

When Daniel and his friends were taken to Babylon, their names were changed. Following is a chart showing their Hebrew names with their meanings versus the names the Babylonians gave them. I find this a very interesting display of how obviously opposite the Hebrews were from the

Chapter 18

Babylonians.

Hebrew Names	Meanings	Babylonian Names	Meanings
Daniel	God is my Judge	became Belteshazzar	Bel will protect
Hananiah	Yah* has been gracious	became Shadrach	Inspired by Aku
Mishael	Who is what God is?	became Meshach	Belonging to Aku
Azariah	Yah has helped	became Abednego	Servant of Nego

*a shortened version of Yahweh

Daniel 1:8 says Daniel and his three friends <u>resolved</u> not to defile themselves with the Babylonian food, and God blessed them for their faithfulness.

◯ Daniel 1 (Read the whole chapter!)

◯ NOTE: The Book of Daniel is 12 chapters long. The first 6 chapters are the actual story of Daniel, and the last 6 are prophecies, dreams, and prayers. We will be reading through the first 6 chapters throughout this week. Today, only read the first chapter. As you read through this wonderful story, make sure you ask your child to narrate each chapter/section.

Narration Break: retell the wonderful start to the story of Daniel.

Shortly after Daniel and his friends were brought to Babylon, King Nebuchadnezzar was troubled by a dream he could not remember or understand. He was so flustered by this dream, he called every wiseman, astrologer, and magician to interpret his dream. He threatened them with their lives if they could not tell the dream and its meaning. Not a single one of them could tell him the dream or unravel the meaning. King Nebuchadnezzar was completely overwhelmed with anger. He commanded that all the wisemen of the kingdom be executed. When Daniel heard this, he and his friends prayed all night. God heard them, and He gave Daniel the answer in a vision. Daniel was taken to the king, and said...

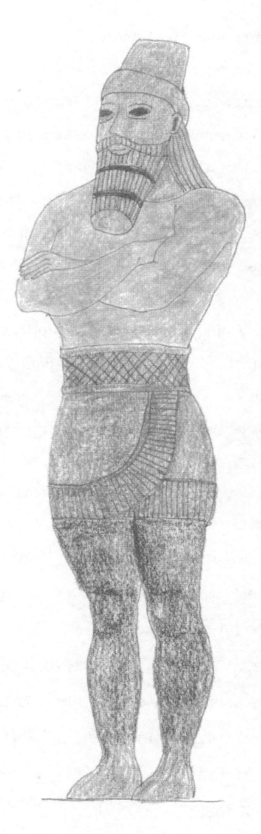

"Oh king, no man, whether he be a magician or wise-man, could tell you the mystery which you have asked. The only One who can reveal to you this mystery is the God of Heaven. He reveals mysteries, and He has shown you what is to happen in days to come. Oh king, as you were lying there trying to sleep, God showed you what is going to happen to your kingdom and to the kingdoms which will follow. I am not telling you these things because I am greater in wisdom than other men, but because God has allowed me to know so that I may tell you.

As you were looking, O king, there, before you stood a dazzling statue of enormous height, which was awesome in appearance. The head of the statue was made of pure gold, its chest and arms were formed by silver, its belly and thighs of bronze, its legs of iron, and its feet partly of iron and partly of baked clay.

As you were watching, a Rock was cut, but not by human hands. It came and struck the statue on its feet and smashed them. At this time, the iron, the clay, the bronze, the silver, and the gold were broken all to pieces and became like chaff which the wind swept away without leaving a single trace. And the Rock, which struck the statue, remained and became a huge mountain that filled the entire earth.

This, O king, is the meaning of your dream: you, King Nebuchadnezzar, are the head of gold. God has given you dominion and power and glory. After you, there will arise another kingdom, which will be inferior to yours. Next, the third kingdom will arise. This kingdom of bronze will rule the entire earth. Finally, a fourth kingdom will arise. This kingdom will be as strong as iron. This iron kingdom will smash everything in its way to set up its reign in the earth. The feet, which you saw were iron mixed with clay, will be partly strong and partly brittle. The people of this kingdom will be mixed and will remain divided. It will be during this time that the God of Heaven will set up a kingdom that will last forever. It will never be destroyed. This is the meaning of the Rock not cut by human hands. This Rock will destroy all of the other kingdoms." (This is my personal paraphrase of Daniel 2: 27-45)

After Daniel had told King Nebuchadnezzar the dream and the meaning, the king fell to the floor in front of him. He declared that the God who enabled Daniel to tell the dream and its meaning was surely the God of all. The king also placed Daniel and his friends in positions of power in Babylon. You would think King Nebuchadnezzar would not soon forget the power of God, but it was not long before he was getting a big head.

It makes me chuckle... I don't know if King Nebuchadnezzar was trying to build a statue like the one in his dream, but he had a ninety foot tall statue built and placed in the most conspicuous place he could. Maybe old King Nebuchadnezzar had lain awake at night trying to figure out how he could make the dream not come true! After all, God had said that he was only the "golden head" of the dream statue. Maybe he thought building a statue completely out of gold and making everyone bow to it would change the outcome. Take the time now to read what happened next...

☻ Daniel 3 (Read the entire account of what happened.)

☻ Daniel 4 (Please read what happened to King Nebuchadnezzar next.)

To finish up our chapter together, we need to look in on Daniel again. He is twenty-three years older than the last time we met up with him. The Babylonian king on the throne was Belshazzar. Look back at the Babylonian name given to Daniel when he arrived there. Do you see how close it is to this king's name? Make sure you do not confuse them!

King Belshazzar was what we call a co-regent with his father, Nabonidus. They were not a good pair. It seems King Nabonidus was more interested in archaeology than in ruling the kingdom, and King Belshazzar was a lazy, evil man. Daniel chapter 5 opens on the scene of a party being given by Belshazzar. This was not a nice, quiet, simple party. I will not go into details about what kind of party this was for the sake of my youngest friends hearing this story, but I will say King Belshazzar did not have any idea of what lines he was crossing.

Daniel 5:2 says that the king ordered that the gold and silver drinking vessels from God's house be brought to him. Remember, these are the holy vessels that Nebuchadnezzar had taken when he plundered Judah. So here was this slovenly, evil king of Babylon laying intoxicated on his couch, misusing the sacred vessels of God. Not only did these drunken Babylonians drink their wine out of the vessels, but they toasted the false gods of Babylon with them. I shudder to think what God was doing right at that moment. I can imagine The Ancient of Days coming to His feet in a Holy fury. Suddenly, everyone at the king's party screamed in terror. As they watched with white, horror-stricken faces, a huge, human hand appeared and wrote these words on the wall: MENE, MENE, TEKEL, PARSIN, which means: MENE - God has numbered the days of your reign and brought it to an end. TEKEL- You have been weighed on the scales and found wanting. PARSIN- Your kingdom is divided and given to the Medes and Persians.

The golden head of the dream statue was about to crash to the ground. The Babylonians had become complacent in their security, and they believed that they were untouchable and unconquerable. God was about to prove them wrong; that very night, Belshazzar was killed, and Darius the Mede took over the kingdom.

The wall surrounding Babylon was thought to be un-breachable, and the city had enough food laid up for at least twenty years. The great Euphrates River ran through the city, guaranteeing a never-ending water source. So how did the enemy get in? They dug a canal to divert enough of the river to create a space to get in through the water gates. The Babylonians never saw them coming. The "silver chest and arms" kingdom had arrived.

◌ Please read any remaining verses of Daniel chapters 1-6.

Narration Break: retell the story of the fall of Babylon. Read

"*Apologetics through Archaeology*" # 17 & 18.

Interesting Note: During the time of Daniel, there lived mighty prophets of the Lord. One of these prophets was named Jeremiah. Daniel read the prophecies of Jeremiah and knew, while he himself would probably die in exile, his people would be freed. In our previous chapter, we looked at the major prophets of Israel and Judah who lived during the time of the divided kingdom of Israel. One of these prophets was Isaiah. Read Isaiah 45:1- 4. Isaiah wrote this prophecy 150 years before Cyrus was born. It would be Cyrus the Medo-Persian who would release the Hebrews to return to their homeland.

Esther... For such a time as this

Ezra 1:1-4, 7

"In the first year of Cyrus king of Persia, in order to fulfill the word of the Lord spoken by Jeremiah, the Lord moved the heart of Cyrus king of Persia to make a proclamation throughout his realm and also to put it in writing:

2 "This is what Cyrus king of Persia says: 'The Lord, the God of heaven, has given me all the kingdoms of the earth and he has appointed me to build a temple for him at Jerusalem in Judah. 3 Any of his people among you may go up to Jerusalem in Judah and build the temple of the Lord, the God of Israel, the God who is in Jerusalem, and may their God be with them. 4 And in any locality where survivors may now be living, the people are to provide them with silver and gold, with goods and livestock, and with freewill offerings for the temple of God in Jerusalem.'"

7 Moreover, King Cyrus brought out the articles belonging to the temple of the Lord, which Nebuchadnezzar had carried away from Jerusalem and had placed in the temple of his god."

Thus started the return of the exiles to Jerusalem, but it was not an easy process. Many of the returning Jews had never seen Jerusalem and only knew it by the accounts passed down throughout the generations. The rubble pile, which was all that was left of the once-beautiful wall surrounding their beloved city, was a far cry from what they expected. A young man from the line of David was sent to govern the people as they rebuilt the walls. The rebuilding project would go on for over a century.

◯ Read about what happened in Ezra 3:8 - 4:24.

Not all of the Jews taken into Babylon were eager to return to Jerusalem. Some of them were quite comfortable and wealthy. Many of them had married Babylonian spouses and had several generations of children and grandchildren. Some of them held prominent positions in the Babylonian government. Amongst the Hebrews who decided to stay in Babylon, was a man named Mordecai, the grandson of Kish, who had been carried away from Jerusalem, when King Nebuchadnezzar had invaded.

Mordecai had raised his much younger, orphaned cousin, Hadassah (hu-DAS-u). We know this young woman by her Persian name, Esther, and her story is one of the most fascinating of all Bible stories. (The Book of Esther is found before Job, which, of course, means that the Bible is not in chronological order.) Esther, as we are learning, took place after the Book of Daniel, and like the story of Daniel, Esther affords us a wonderful glimpse into two worlds at once, the Persian and the Jewish.

This intriguing story opens with the words, "Now it came to pass in the days of Ahasuerus..." This kind of beginning to a story in Ancient Hebrew is similar to our "Once upon a time, in a far away land..." And what a story it is, too, having all of the elements of a superb fairytale... a king, a vile villain, a queen scorned and sent away forever, and, of course, a young orphaned girl - ripped from her home and shoved into the limelight of queen-hood.

Allow me to introduce the cast members in today's story...

The king in the story, Ahasuerus, also called Xerxes, was the grandson of Cyrus the Great. Xerxes was noble and of royal blood. It is said that he was tall, handsome, and, dare we say, just a wee bit spoiled? After all, he was the king of the great Persian Empire, and he was used to getting his own way!

◉ Read Esther 1

The villain in the story, Haman, was King Xerxes's trusted advisor and confidant. If you remember back to our story of Israel's first king, Saul, you will remember that he disobeyed God's command to kill all of the Amalekites. Agag was the king of the Amalekites and one of Haman's ancestors. Haman, who knew his peoples' history, hated the Jews. He especially hated Mordecai, because Mordecai refused to bow to him. He wanted nothing more than to annihilate the Jewish people from the face of the earth.

Read Esther 2

Vashti, the queen who disobeyed the king and was banished, has a short but important role in our story. What followed her banishment was a plan, which God deftly orchestrated to fulfill His purposes. Evil was afoot, and He knew that He would need someone in place to step forward to do what He commanded.

Hadassah, a young, beautiful, Jewish woman, was chosen above all the other maidens brought to the palace for the king. Although God knew she was beautiful to look upon, He was looking at her heart, her love for her people, and her willingness to obey Him, even when it meant she could lose her life.

When Hadassah came to the palace with the other young, unmarried women, she was being taken from everything she knew and held dear. Her guardian, Mordecai, sat at the gates and listened for word about his beloved cousin. He was a God-fearing Hebrew, who had brought his ward up in the knowledge of all traditions the Jewish people held dear. I have to wonder what these two were thinking. I am sure that they prayed to the God of Heaven Who had delivered their ancestors from the Egyptians. They had to trust that He had a reason for letting this happen.

It was not long after Hadassah, renamed Esther, became queen, that Mordecai, sitting in his usual place at the palace gate, overheard a plot to kill the king. Mordecai sent word to Esther, who in turn told the king. The two conspirators, who were officials of the court, were hung on the gallows. It was entered into the records that Mordecai had heard and reported the scheme, and that he should be given a reward. Of course this made Haman even more angry. Oh, how he hated this stubborn Jew!

Narration Break: discuss our story so far.

I love the character of Mordecai in this story. His stubborn refusal to bow to Haman reminds me of some other godly people who resolved to live out their godly convictions in the face of danger. Just like Joseph, who refused to sin when Potiphar's wife demanded it, and like Daniel, who would not eat the food God had said not to eat, or his friends, who would not bow to King Nebuchadnezzar's golden statue, Mordecai would not bow. All of these Biblical characters are examples of God's care for those who trust and obey Him. Sometimes we are determined to do the right thing, and it angers those who are living evil lives around us. This is what Mordecai's very presence did to Haman; it rankled him.

Haman was like all other evil bigots. (A bigot is a person who hates the members of a certain people group for reasons based on evil and prejudice.) He hated the Jews so much, he planned to inflict upon them a holocaust of vast proportions. Haman fumed and schemed until he had a plan he thought the king would give into. He went to King Xerxes and filled his ears with lies about the Jews living in Persia. Read the following Scripture to see what happened.

Esther 3: 5-15

Perhaps King Xerxes was feeling pressure to rebuild his kingdom after the ill-fated wars with the Greeks because he was easily persuaded to let Haman have his way with the Jews in Persia. He was most grateful that Haman was so trustworthy in handling the inside affairs of the kingdom. The last sentence of Esther, chapter 3, says the king and Haman sat down to have a drink while the the rest of the city of Susa was bewildered.

I can imagine that the residents of Susa were bewildered! The edict proclaimed that there were eleven months before the Jews would be completely destroyed. The terror of waiting would play some pretty nasty tricks on their minds, and Haman knew this. Just when we think Haman is going to have the upper hand and the last say, let's look at something wonderful, something that will remind all of us that God has all of the timing worked out.

Remember what you read in Esther 3:7? Haman cast a lot to see when the annihilation of the Jews should happen. The lots were cast on the "twelfth year...in the first month." Now read verse 12 of the same

chapter. What exact day was the edict drafted? It was drafted on the thirteenth day of the first month. Now read Leviticus 23:4-5.

"⁴These are the feasts of the LORD, even holy convocations, which ye shall proclaim in their seasons. ⁵In the fourteenth day of the first month at even is the LORD'S passover."

Do you see the connection? The news couriers were strategically placed throughout the kingdom to deliver whatever proclamations the king made. This means, Haman's evil edict would have been delivered on the first day of the Passover. Let this sink in for a moment. The Feast of Passover was the remembrance of God's protection of the Israelites from the angel of death, who killed all of the firstborn in Egypt.

When Mordecai received the news of the edict, he tore his clothes and piled ashes on his head. He wept and wailed so loudly that Esther sent a messenger down to see what was the matter with him. When she was informed of the calamitous edict, Esther was in agony and implored Mordecai to tell her what she should do about it. Read Mordecai's response in chapter 4:7-16...

7 Mordecai told him everything that had happened to him, including the exact amount of money Haman had promised to pay into the royal treasury for the destruction of the Jews. 8 He also gave him a copy of the text of the edict for their annihilation, which had been published in Susa, to show to Esther and explain it to her, and he told him to instruct her to go into the king's presence to beg for mercy and plead with him for her people.

9 Hathak went back and reported to Esther what Mordecai had said. 10 Then she instructed him to say to Mordecai, 11 "All the king's officials and the people of the royal provinces know that for any man or woman who approaches the king in the inner court without being summoned the king has but one law: that they be put to death unless the king extends

the gold scepter to them and spares their lives. But thirty days have passed since I was called to go to the king."

12 When Esther's words were reported to Mordecai, 13 he sent back this answer: "Do not think that because you are in the king's house you alone of all the Jews will escape. 14 For if you remain silent at this time, relief and deliverance for the Jews will arise from another place, but you and your father's family will perish. And who knows but that you have come to your royal position for such a time as this?"

15 Then Esther sent this reply to Mordecai: 16 "Go, gather together all the Jews who are in Susa, and fast for me. Do not eat or drink for three days, night or day. I and my attendants will fast as you do. When this is done, I will go to the king, even though it is against the law. And if I perish, I perish."

So, after three days of fasting and praying, Esther went before the king without invitation. This took more courage than you or I can imagine, because there was a law which said no one, not even the queen, could appear before the King without being summoned. Esther 5:2 says when the king saw Esther, she found favor in his sight.

◉Read what happened next in Esther 6 - 7

It was in this way, the motive for Haman's evil plot to annihilate the Jews was revealed. The king was so angry that he took all of Haman's properties and gave them to Esther. Mordecai was placed in a position of honor and influence, and the Jews were saved.

Narration Break: retell the story of Esther and how God used her to fulfill His plan. Read "Apologetics through Archaeology" #19.

Early American Cultures

We learned earlier that after the Tower of Babel, groups of people wandered in every direction from the Fertile Crescent. Many groups wandered over the Bering Land Bridge, into the Americas. Others may have come over on Phoenician trade ships.

We call these people Ancient Americans, even though this is not what they called themselves. We do not have written records from these early Americans, but we have learned a fair amount from the artifacts they left behind. We know they discovered the use of rock and animal bones for weapons. We also know that various tribes were skilled hunters, while other tribes were successful farmers.

We have learned, from the artifact "trails," that people groups eventually traveled all the way to the southern tip of South America. Of course these continents were not called the Americas until much later, when a European explorer, named Amerigo Vespucci, declared South America to be a "new" continent. The people who lived there were dubbed "Indian" by European explorers of the late A.D 1400's and early 1500's.

Many do not know that people, in the Eastern Hemisphere, even knew the existence of the vast Western continents. However, historians agree, there were many traders from the Orient, who were well aware of the presence of their neighbors across the Pacific. Many Chinese junks set anchor in harbors along the western coast of, what would become, the United States of America. Because of the closed nature of the government in China (among other countries of the Orient), we do not know the extent of the trading that happened pre-European explorer days.

These early American tribes of people lived in various ways, but most of them had one thing in common - they were mostly nomadic. For example, the groups who lived in the far Northern regions of the continent hunted and fished to survive. Their housing material depended upon the climate of where they lived. They made their homes from ice, and their fires from whale blubber oil.

The tribes living a little further south, in the middle of North America, used heavy animal furs, attached to sturdy wooden poles, to construct snug abodes. These mid-North American tribes also depended heavily upon the wildlife and farming for their survival, and they were quite adept at these skills. They grew corn and wheat and hunted the great, roaming herds of buffalo. The buffalo also provided them with clothing, blankets, and weapon.

Tribes of the desert lived in caves. Like the Northern tribe, they hunted for survival, but the desert tribes mostly hunted wild sheep to eat. These tribes were also known for their beautiful basket weaving, and there have been artifacts found, indicating that they made interesting clothing and footwear with intricate beading and feathering.

In the area, which we call Central America, lived a tribe called the Olmecs. They were the first civilization in Central America, and they are one of the most well-known of the Ancient Central Americans. The Olmecs built something amazing - a giant city. This city, which we now call San Lorenzo, was built in the country now called Mexico. The Olmecs built their giant city on a huge hill, and in the middle of their city was a gigantic pyramid. The Olmecs built this pyramid out of sand and clay, in the same way the Ancient Egyptians built their pyramids - by hand and one block at a time. At the very top of this pyramid was a temple for the Olmecs' gods. The temple and pyramid have long since worn away and disappeared, but there was something that has lasted through the centuries.

Look at the picture on the left. What do you think this is? This is a

drawing of one of the Olmec heads. These strange statues sit around the area that used to be the base of the Olmecs' giant pyramid temple. No one knows for sure what they are for or what they are supposed to be, but most historians think they are statues in honor of the Olmecs' most famous rulers. These giant heads are about nine feet tall!

Narration Break: discuss what we have learned so far.

It seems the further south you go on the continent of South America, the more mysterious the ancient civilizations became. South American tribes had strange cultures which are mysterious even today. We know from artifacts, many of the tribes living there practiced many peculiar, and rather bizarre religious ceremonies. Most of them believed in witchcraft and had "medicine men" who held powerful positions in the tribes.

One tribe in particular has remained exceptionally mysterious. The Nazca (NAZ-cu) lived in the area which is now Peru. This ancient tribe, which has not been around for more than two thousand years, left behind something so incredibly strange that it has left historians and archaeologists scratching their heads in bewilderment.

About two thousand years after the Nazca had disappeared, a pilot flying a plane over that area, discovered gigantic drawings scratched into the earth. These drawings cover miles and miles of ground. The drawings are not visible in their entirety when standing on the ground; they simply look like old roads or deep ruts in the earth. You have to be hundreds of feet up in the air to see the whole drawing at one time. How did the Nazca do this?

Whenever people are trying to keep God out of the story of humanity, they try to come up with an explanation for how something happened. This is why the theory of Evolution is so popular, it removes the need for a Creator. If we are all here on the earth as a result of big bang somewhere up in the Cosmos, then what is the real purpose in life? If we are the result of an explosion, with no created purpose, then there is no reason to have hope. If God is not real, then Jesus is not real. Without Jesus, we have no hope, and we are just walking around

here on earth, with no reason for joy. I don't know about you, but I could not live like that! I need to know I was created for a purpose, and I need to know God has a great plan for me. I do not want to explain away God's obvious involvement in the history of the world.

We see this type of "explaining away" when it comes to the Nazca lines and ground drawings. Many people believe these symbols were created by aliens who came to earth, from other planets, millions of years ago and "planted" the human race here. How do people come up with ideas like this? Some of the explanation they give points to some skulls that have been found in what used to be part of the great Nazca and Incan civilizations.

These skulls are elongated and grotesquely deformed, very similar in shape to the "traditional" science fiction alien heads. However, historians and archaeologists have discovered that these ancient people groups performed ritual head wrapping on infants, which resulted in these

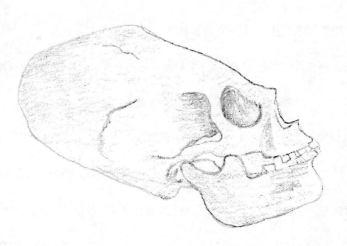

misshapen heads. This practice was also prominent in many other civilizations; elongated skulls like these have been found in Northern Asia, Southern Africa, and on Egyptian mummies.

Another explanation, and completely plausible reason for the amazing ground drawings has been uncovered by the discovery of artifacts and research of the Nazca civilization; the Nazca people were extremely advanced in mathematics and astronomy. Their study of the sky, using lenses and ocular devices, shows us that they used the stars, in their courses across the sky, to measure and tell time.

South American ancient civilizations were steeped in witchcraft and mysterious pagan rituals. The Incan Civilization, which ruled most of the area along the western coast of the continent, is shrouded in mystery. One of their most important cities was a citadel, which was discovered in 1911, by an American historian named Hiram Bingham. Its location had remained a secret for about five hundred years, and its discovery set the the world abuzz.

This lost city of the Incas, Machu Picchu (MACH-oo PEE-coo), is situated high in the lofty heights of the Andes Mountains. This ancient city, with its elaborate stone work and trellised gardens, was once the hub of the Incan Empire. As archaeologists uncovered the ruins, the picture of the Incan lifestyle came into focus, a civilization which lived in fear of the gods: the god of the cosmos, the god of the mountain, and the god of the underworld. Temples and altars, where gruesome sacrifices were made to appease the gods, were discovered at the very highest point of this mountaintop kingdom.

All of these rituals and sacrifices, to appease the gods, are yet another example of the longing, deep inside every human being, to have a mediator. This longing, which is caused by separation from our Creator, has been in every human soul since the Fall. The study of these ancient people should encourage us to see the same longing in the world around us. Take time to celebrate the hope of Jesus today.

Narration Break: talk about the what you have learned. "Apologetics through Archaeology" #20 and the Deeper Research topic for older children go together for this chapter.

Alexander the Great

We have learned the Persian Empire was powerful and ruled a large area of land. Greece, which we learned about earlier in our story, was across the Aegean Sea from Persia. Even though Greece was considered to be a united empire, they did not serve one king like the Persians did. Each of their city-states had their own king.

Athens and Sparta were the two main city states. These two city-states were extremely different, and they fought about everything. Athens was democratic and voted on their laws. They liked learning and deep thinking. They studied the stars and excelled in mathematics. The Athenians were very philosophical. Plato, one of the most famous philosophers of the ancient world, came from Athens. On the other hand, Spartans were rough and tough. They were trained from a very young age to be warriors. Sports and fighting techniques were of top importance.

Then one day, the Persian King Cyrus (you remember him: he sent the Jews back to Jerusalem) decided to take over Greece. He sent messages to Athens and Sparta, to tell them that he would like to make them part of the great Persian empire. He asked them to send him some earth and water, to signify that they would give up without a fight. Of course, this just made them mad. They decided to stop fighting each other and help each other fight the Persians.

What followed was a series of fierce battles between Persia and Greece. King Cyrus was used to defeating everyone who came against him, but these tough Greek warriors gave him quite a fight! This war against Persian invasion started around 500 B.C. and went on for many years.

One of the most famous battles in this war was the Battle of Marathon. One day, news reached Athens that the Persians were crossing the Aegean Sea, with the intention of attacking the small port town of Marathon. The people of Athens panicked, because the Spartans were observing a holiday and would not come to help until the holiday was over. Determined not to let the Persians win, the men of Athens and Marathon marched down to meet the invasion. They bravely charged the Persian army, showered them with arrows, and drove them away.

When they knew that they had won the battle, they sent a runner back to the city of Athens with the news. This runner, Pheidippides (fy-DIP-u-dees), ran a little over twenty-six miles to deliver the message. The legend says that Pheidippides delivered the message and then died of exhaustion. To this day, there is a race, which is a bit over twenty-six miles long, called the marathon. The Battle of Marathon did not end the war between Greece and Persia. The war continued until 480 B.C., when the Greeks finally defeated the Persians, once and for all, in the Battle of Salamis.

You would think that, after fighting the Persians together for so many years, the Spartans and Athenians would forget their old issues, which had caused them to fight before. For a while, they did live in peace, and they built beautiful buildings and restored some of their former culture, but the quiet did not last long. Instead of living peacefully together in their country, they became more and more jealous and fearful of each other. Why did they do this? They were each afraid that the other was becoming more powerful, so they started attacking each other again. We call this war, between Sparta and Athens, the Pelopponesian (pel-o-pu-NEE-shun) War, and it raged on and on for twenty-five years!

Finally, Sparta took over Athens after a long siege which ended when Athens was betrayed by one of their own. Athens had fallen prey to a deadly plague, in which a vast multitude of people had died. Both Athens and Sparta were worn down and weak after their long rivalry. Many of the men were dead, leaving their country in a weakened condition and open for the invasion which was heading their way.

Narration Break: talk about the story so far.

Someone had been watching the Athenians and Spartans fighting each other until they were both weak. To the north of Greece was the country of Macedonia (mas-u-DOE-nee-u), which was ruled by a king name Phillip. King Phillip decided to take advantage of the weakened state of the Greeks. Soon, Greece was under the control of Macedonia, and Phillip set his eyes to the east. He wanted to attack and conquer the great Persian Empire, but this was not to be. King Phillip died before he was able to follow through with his plan. After Phillip died, his son, Alexander, took the throne.

Alexander was even more eager than his father had been to attack the Persians. The Persians may not have been able to conquer the Greeks, but they were still the biggest empire on earth at the time. Their vast empire stretched from Asia Minor to India. Alexander was intent on conquering it all and ruling the entire world. Alexander, which means "the ruler of men," would become known throughout history as Alexander the Great. No other ruler, up to that time in history, had ever marched into and conquered as many empires.

Do you remember our story about Daniel? Do you remember the dream that King Nebuchadnezzar had about the giant statue? You have added onto your "dream statue" when a new empire has taken its place, just like God showed in the dream. You are about to see the Bronze Kingdom take its place. Under the rule of Alexander the Great, the Greek (and his original Macedonian) Empire became the next mighty empire to rule the known world.

Alexander conquered the rest of Persia and wanted to go into India. However, when he invaded, Alexander quickly found out that the Indian warriors were skilled warriors. After his men refused to keep fighting in India, Alexander was forced to retreat and concentrate on ruling his

This drawing of Alexander the Great was taken from a famous fresco made in his likeness.

huge empire.

Alexander also marched down into Egypt and conquered them. He was made the Pharaoh of Egypt and ordered a city built in his honor. Alexandria, Egypt was built near the river delta, where the Nile empties into the Mediterranean Sea. Even though Alexander helped plan the city, he died before he could see the buildings. Alexandria is still an important city today. It is a center for art, higher learning, and culture. Outside the city of Alexandria, a giant lighthouse was erected, to help guide ships into the port of the city. This lighthouse was the biggest in the world and stood well over three hundred feet high. Although the lighthouse is no longer there, Alexandria is still an important coastal city, where many ships from around the world visit.

Alexander's reign started when he was only twenty years old, and it took him the next eleven years to spread his kingdom. It is said that Alexander was depressed when he had no other conquests to make. He ruled the majority of the known world, but yet he was miserable. Alexander's rule was cut short when he contracted a mysterious disease and died at the age of 32. He was buried in Alexandria, Egypt.

After his death, Alexander's vast empire was split between three of his generals. One of the generals ruled Macedonia and the northern portion of the kingdom in Asia Minor. Another general, named Ptolemy (TOLL-u-me), became the ruler of Egypt. It was under Ptolemy's rule that the city of Alexandria was finished. Ptolemy also insured that the library at Alexandria was filled with books about culture and art. The last section of the empire was given to the third general, Seleucus (su-LOO-sus), to rule. This area, which is now called Syria, included the southern part of Asia, spreading easterly almost to India. Of course, these three generals did not get along. Each wanted to be the strongest, and so, over the next century, there was much fighting amongst them. In our next chapter, we will see the empire which would be the legs of iron.

Narration Break: talk about the rest of the story. Read "Apologetics through Archaeology" #21.

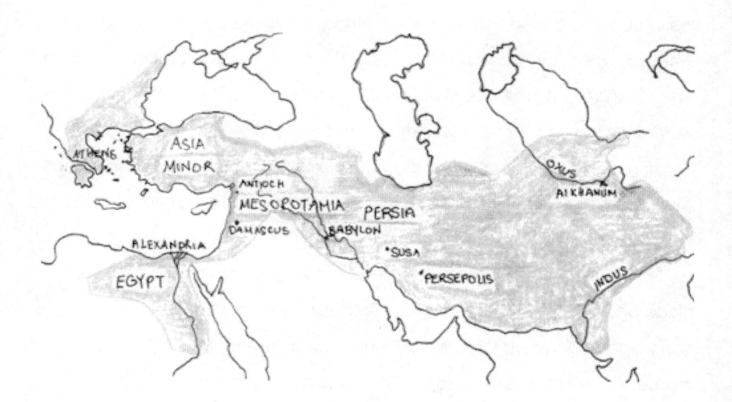

Alexander the Great's Kingdom

The Rise of the Roman Empire

Our story has wound around the entire world and has come back to rest in the "Cradle of Civilization" - the Middle East. In our last two chapters, we have learned about the mysterious civilizations of the early Americas and the conquests of Alexander the Great, which encompassed most of the known world. In this chapter, we are going to learn about the next "superpower" kingdom of the ancient world. As we learned, when we studied about King Nebuchadnezzar's dream, kingdom after kingdom would rise and fall. Babylon, the "golden head" kingdom, was overthrown by the "silver chest and arms" kingdom, the Medo-Persians. The "bronze belly and thighs" kingdom was ushered in when Alexander the Great spread the Greek Empire over the map as far as he could.

Now it is time to see how the "iron legs" kingdom would take its place on the timeline of prophecy fulfilled. I want you to go back to our story about Daniel in Chapter 18 and look at the picture of the dream statue. As we start at the top of the statue, and move through the kingdoms signified by the different metals, notice that each metal is stronger than the one before it. Gold is worth the most but also the easiest to bend and mold. While silver is worth less, it is stronger than gold. Bronze is next in order, as well as in value, for both gold and silver are worth much more. However, bronze is stronger than both gold and

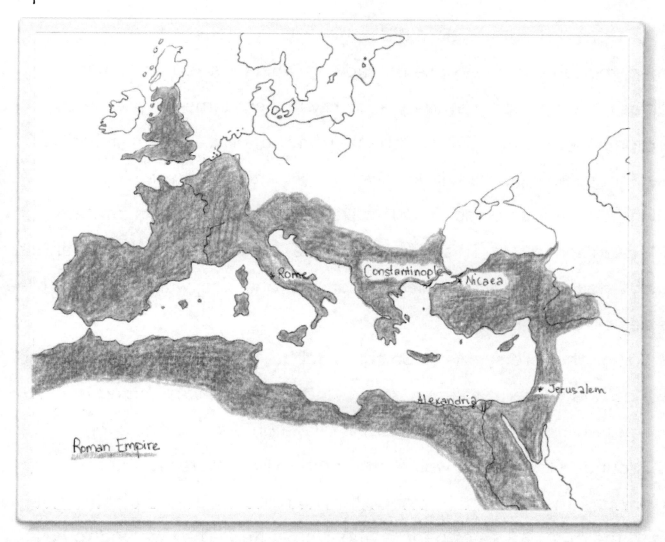

Roman Empire

silver, like the Greek kingdom was stronger than the Babylonian and the Medo-Persian kingdoms. Another kingdom was coming, however, and this one would be immeasurably stronger than those that preceded it.

The great kingdom of Alexander had been divided up between his three generals. We learned that these men did not get along, and of course, they were all jealous and nervous about each other's greatness and power. They all wanted to be the strongest, so they fought against each other.

Chapter 22

Our next great kingdom did not develop because of one of these men, though. Unlike Greece or Babylon, which started from many big cities united or conquered by a mighty leader, Rome started as an insignificant town, which sat on one of seven hills. This small, and seemingly unimportant, little town, was situated on a seemingly unimportant little piece of land, called Italy, that juts down into the Mediterranean Sea. This type of land mass is called a peninsula, and it is only attached to a larger piece of land on one side, with the other three sides bordered by water.

Though there seems to be some debate on the beginning of Rome, we do know, one of the first seven kings of Rome was named Romulus. Rome, which started out as a small village on one hill, was soon surrounded by other towns on the other hills. Eventually, the towns all grew together to form a larger city. The rulers of these cities fought with the other tribes of people who lived in Italy. They wanted to have more room to make a more powerful kingdom.

One of these tribes was the Etruscan (i-TRU-skun) tribe. They were the most powerful of the tribes and caused the most trouble for the kings. The Etruscans were farmers, tradesmen, and artists who liked to trade with the Greeks. They learned a lot from the Greeks, which soon became part of their culture, and they passed along the Greeks' way of doing things, such as their clothing style. They also learned how to read and write the Greek language. All of this Greek influence, in the Etruscan lives, eventually trickled down to the Romans.

The Etruscans also adopted and passed along the Greeks' false gods. The Romans called the gods by their own names and made up myths and legends about them. We are not going to fill our story with such legends and myths about false gods; simply understand that the Romans, like the Greeks, were polytheists. As Rome conquered more and more of the tribes who surrounded them, they eventually ruled the entire peninsula of Italy.

As the Roman Empire grew and spread out, they built amazing road systems between the major cities. These roadways were extremely advanced for that time period and, in some cases, may still be used today! The Romans were also famous for their ingenious water transporting systems. These aqueducts, as they were called, brought fresh water into the cities, making it possible for the people to have enough water without digging wells.

The Ancient Romans were not known to be gentle. On the contrary, they were bloodthirsty and violent. An example of this would be one of their favorite sports - watching gladiator matches. Gladiators were muscular and strong, and they were trained from a young age to fight and kill, with a sword and with their hands. People gathered in large, outdoor stadiums to watch gladiators fight each other. It was a gruesome event to watch!

Narration Break: talk about what you have learned so far about the Romans.

As the Roman Empire spread through conquest, they became a threat to the other civilizations around them. Do you remember when we learned about the Phoenicians? They were traders and shipbuilders, and they were known for their beautiful carving, shipbuilding, and unique purple dye made from Murex snail. The Phoenicians had built a city, called Carthage, on the northern edge of Africa, across the Mediterranean Sea from Italy. They were concerned that the Romans would soon be in control of all the Mediterranean Sea passages, which would be detrimental to their trade. Of course, the Carthaginians could not have this, and the Romans would not accept that they could not control the Mediterranean Sea, so of course, they fought each other.

For over a hundred years, the Carthaginians and the Romans fought. We call these wars the Punic Wars, and they started in 264 B.C. and went to 146 B.C. Most of these battles took place on the sea, but a few times, each side invaded each others' main cities.

The Carthaginian general, Hannibal, invaded Italy in 218 B.C. by taking elephants around the Mediterranean Sea by land. He brought his army up and around through the mountains in Northern Italy. He had great victory on his rampage. He burned down cities and farms and killed many Roman citizens. When the Romans found out about Hannibal's rampage, they went into the city of Carthage and attacked when the Carthaginians were least expecting. When Hannibal heard this, he brought his men back home to help, but his army was so exhausted from their plundering in Italy, that they did not win the battle. Rome now had the upper hand, and soon they had conquered the city of Carthage. Rome had finally won.

The Romans had changed their government from a dictatorship to a Consul government, which means there were now two rulers of Rome. They did not want only one man to have the power over the entire Empire. It was at this time that there was a young man named Julius Caesar. He idolized Alexander the Great and wanted to become the ruler of the Roman Empire. Through a strange chain of events, Julius was sent by the Consul to govern the Roman Empire's lands in Spain. This made him angry, and he determined that he would become the ruler of all the Romans.

Finally, Julius Caesar was allowed to return to Rome, and he convinced the Consul to let him become the third member. The Consul was supposed to listen to the Senate, which was a select group of wealthy and powerful men. However, Julius Caesar was not the kind of person who wanted to listen to anyone. He was determined to be the supreme power of Rome, and he knew how to get that position; he made himself extremely popular with the people. Like so many other manipulating political leaders in history, Caesar won the masses with his exemplary oratorial skills. In other words, he was a smooth talker, and soon, he had the hearts of his fellow Romans.

Julius decided the only way for him to become the ruler of Rome was if he conquered other lands, so out he marched with his army. He decided to march north, build ships, and attack Britain. Do you remember when we learned about the Celts who lived in Britain and Northern Europe? They were warriors who were proud of their ability to fight, and when the Romans landed in Britain, the Celts kept them from conquering all their land. Even though the Senate and Consul tried to

have Caesar arrested and executed for treason, they could not get rid of him because the people loved and admired him.

On one of his conquests, Julius Caesar marched down to Egypt, intending to conquer it, but instead he fell in love with the queen of Egypt. Queen Cleopatra was quite beautiful and used her charms to convince the great Roman ruler to help her get rid of her brother, who was supposed to be co-ruler of Egypt. By promising Caesar a share of her wealth, Cleopatra manipulated the greatest and strongest Roman.

The Senate feared Caesar, but they could do nothing to stop him, and soon he was the dictator of the Roman Empire. To make sure that his family remained rulers of Rome, Caesar adopted his nephew Octavian, and demanded the Senate make him king after Julius Caesar's death. Of course, the Senate did not want to do this, so they schemed to kill Caesar on the fifteenth of March. When Caesar came to the Senate that day, they attacked him and stabbed him. One of these men was named Brutus; he had been a good friend of Caesar's in years past. As Caesar died, he said in Latin, "Et tu, Brute?" which means, "You too, Brutus?" And so Caesar died there on the floor of the Senate building, killed by his fellow countrymen.

After Caesar's death, his nephew Octavian came to power. The people of Rome loved him. Octavian was renamed Augustus Caesar and expanded the Roman Empire even farther.

The Story of Pompeii

Nestled at the foot of an old volcano was a bustling, thriving Roman city. Pompeii had not always been this busy center of enterprise, for it had humble beginnings. Over five hundred years before, farmers from northern Italy had settled here, planted their crops, and built the first wall to protect their little community. As the centuries passed, the town grew in the shadow of the sleeping volcano of Mount Vesuvius. Trees grew green on the slopes of the mountain, and all seemed well.

Then in A.D. 62, the ground began to shake. An earthquake rumbled through the city of Pompeii leaving, in its wake, mass destruction. Many of Pompeii's buildings were completely destroyed. Many people moved away, afraid of another earthquake, but the poor of the city stayed. What else could they do? They had nowhere else to go. Two years later the earth trembled again, destroying more of the buildings.

It was August 24, 79 A.D. The volcano, which had lain quietly sleeping under its blanket of vegetation, erupted, spewing enough ash and lava to completely bury the city at the foot of its slopes. Pompeii was destroyed.

It did not take long for Pompeii to be completely forgotten. New vegetation grew over the ash covering the city, and as each century marched by, any evidence of Pompeii's existence became buried deeper and deeper. It was in 1600, over one thousand, five hundred years after the fatal eruption, that excavation crews uncovered traces of Pompeii. These were not highly trained archaeologists but construction crews, digging a ditch for a canal.

Mount Vesuvius was not finished yet, and in 1631, the volcano once again spewed its ash and lava down onto the area where Pompeii once stood. Fifty years later, workers digging a new well discovered a section of Pompeii's ruins, and over the next one hundred years, archaeologists worked to uncover the forgotten story of Pompeii. What they found was a gruesome but amazing discovery. It seemed by the position of the human remains, that the volcano caught the inhabitants of Pompeii by surprise.

Today, Pompeii is a tourist attraction to people around the world. Thousands of visitors walk through the streets of the city that spent nearly two thousand years beneath the ash, lava, and new growth. They are amazed to see the walls of homes. These are artifacts of a civilization long forgotten and a rare glimpse into what life was like in Ancient Rome.

Narration Break: talk about what you have read today.

Prepare the Way!

My heart is beating a rapid tempo as I prepare to write the next few chapters. Every complete story has a climax - the part of the story that is the absolute high point - and ours is coming! We know the setting of our story is the world which God created. We have seen the conflict of our story as sin came into God's perfect world. Empires have risen and fallen, and the people, who God chose to be the earthly lineage of the Messiah, were led through many trials and tribulations.

We can almost hear the groaning of the souls of mankind as they long for redemption. From His throne, the Ancient of Days stands to His feet; His glory fills the throne room. The angels' praises rise to a deafening crescendo as the King of Kings turns to the Son. The plan, which had been set in place before the beginning of time, is about to be revealed. I hope I can stay seated long enough to write this - I may have to take a break to dance with glee!

Do you remember how Isaiah the Prophet prophesied about Cyrus the

Daniel 7:9

"...and the Ancient of days did sit, whose garment was white as snow, and the hair of His head like the pure wool: His throne was like the fiery flame, and His wheels as burning fire."

Chapter 23

Great, who would set the captive Israelites free, one hundred and fifty years before Cyrus was even born? Isaiah also prophesied about the Messiah, our Savior and Mediator. This story gives me goosebumps because it shows the glory, the majesty, and the supreme power of our God - the Ancient of Days! In Isaiah 53, seven hundred years before the birth of Christ, Isaiah said...

1"Who has believed our message and to whom has the arm of the Lord been revealed?
2 He grew up before him like a tender shoot, and like a root out of dry ground. He had no beauty or majesty to attract us to him, nothing in his appearance that we should desire him.
3 He was despised and rejected by mankind, a man of suffering, and familiar with pain. Like one from whom people hide their faces he was despised, and we held him in low esteem. 4 Surely he took up our pain and bore our suffering, yet we considered him punished by God, stricken by him, and afflicted. 5 But he was pierced for our transgressions, he was crushed for our iniquities; the punishment that brought us peace was on him, and by his wounds we are healed.
6 We all, like sheep, have gone astray, each of us has turned to our own way; and the Lord has laid on him the iniquity of us all. 7 He was oppressed and afflicted, yet he did not open his mouth; he was led like a lamb to the slaughter, and as a sheep before its shearers is silent, so he did not open his mouth. 8 By oppression[a] and judgment he was taken away.
Yet who of his generation protested? For he was cut off from the land of the living; for the transgression of my people he was punished. [b] 9 He was assigned a grave with the wicked, and with the rich in his death, though he had done no violence, nor was any deceit in his mouth.
10 Yet it was the Lord's will to crush him and cause him to suffer, and though the Lord makes[c] his life an offering for sin, he will see his offspring and prolong his days, and the will of the Lord will prosper in his hand. 11 After he has suffered, he will see the light of life[d] and be satisfied[e]; by his knowledge[f] my righteous servant will justify many, and he will bear their iniquities. 12 Therefore I will give him a portion among the great, [g] and he will divide the spoils with the strong, [h] because he poured out his life unto death, and was numbered with the transgressors. For he bore the sin of many, and made intercession for the transgressors.

We know there is a four hundred year span between the stories of the Old Testament and where the New Testament begins. As we have learned, many changes happened between the prophets of Israel, which is the last section of the Old Testament. At this point in our story, we know the Roman Empire, the "iron legs" empire from King Nebuchadnezzar's dream statue, is ruling most of the known world, including the land of Israel.

When Cyrus the Great let the Israelites return to rebuild Jerusalem, they did not become an independent nation right away. They were ruled by various kings until they were able to free themselves and choose their own ruler, the son of a priest. This family ruled Israel until the Romans came and easily conquered the Jews. From that time on, Israel was ruled by the Romans.

The Roman capital was far away from Judah, so the Roman emperor sent a ruler, named Herod, to govern the Jews. Herod was not a good governor, but he wanted the Jews to like him, so he rebuilt their temple in Jerusalem. It was a glorious, marble building, which was partially covered in gold and silver. The Roman government allowed the Hebrews to worship their God and did not interfere with their customs. As long as they paid their taxes to the Roman government, kept the peace, and did not cause division in the Roman empire, they went on with their lives uneventfully. However, there was the underlying knowledge that their beloved city of Jerusalem was occupied by a foreign power.

This is the backdrop for the beginning of the New Testament, which starts with four separate accounts of the life of Jesus while He was here on earth. These accounts were written by friends and followers of Jesus, under the influence of the Holy Spirit. My personal favorite of the four is the Gospel of John. This story has such a special place in my heart, because John was called the "Beloved Disciple." We will be reading from all of the Gospels, as they each cover the story from a slightly different angle.

Narration Break: talk about what we have learned so far.

The prophecy of the Messiah was about to come true, so God sent a messenger on ahead to tell the people to prepare the way. We can read the story about this messenger in the first part of Luke chapter one. We read that an elderly couple was chosen to be the parents of this messenger. The man, Zechariah, was a priest from the priestly division of Abijah, and his wife, Elizabeth, was a descendant of Aaron, the brother of Moses.

Luke 1 tells the story of these two servants of God. The words used to describe them are wonderful, the kind of words I would love God to use to describe me some day. The Scripture says they were "upright in the sight of God" and they "observed all of the Lord's commandments blamelessly."

The next sentence reveals their heartache in life. They were without children. This story makes me a little teary, because it shows how God

blesses those who trust and serve Him. Here were Zechariah and

Elizabeth, serving God together, trusting and loving Him, even though

He had not blessed them with a child. Remember, in those days, if

someone could not have a child, they were considered cursed in some way, and they were looked down upon and rejected by their peers. But just like every plan that God has for those who trust in Him, this one was for a certain time.

One day, Zechariah was fulfilling his duties as a priest, when an angel of the Lord appeared to him. The angel had a message for him from God; he and Elizabeth would have a son! Zechariah had probably given up on ever having children, as he and Elizabeth were quiet advanced in years, and he did not believe the angel. Because of his unbelief, Zechariah could not talk until his son was born.

Zechariah and Elizabeth's son would be become known as John the Baptist. Elizabeth was the cousin of Jesus's mother, so this made John the Baptist Jesus's cousin. The Book of Matthew describes John the Baptist in a rather colorful fashion.

Matthew 3:4

"...John had his raiment of camel's hair, and a leathern girdle about his loins; and his meat was locusts and wild honey."

🌑 Read Matthew 3: 1-12 to learn more about John the Baptist.

In our next chapter, we will learn the story of our Savior's birth. It is, even to this date, the beginning of the most amazing and wonderful event in all of history.

Narration Break: talk about what we have learned about the birth of John the Baptist.

The Word Became Flesh

"In the beginning was the Word, and the Word was with God, and the Word was God. 2 He was with God in the beginning. 3 Through him all things were made; without him nothing was made that has been made." John 1:1-3

The story in this chapter is not something I take lightly because I do not wish to simply tell a story about Jesus, as if His birth was just another historical event. In this and the following chapters, we are going to contemplate the most significant event ever to happen in the history of the world.

The prophet Isaiah said in chapter 60:1-3...

"Arise, shine, for your light has come,
   and the glory of the Lord rises upon you.
2 See, darkness covers the earth
   and thick darkness is over the peoples,
but the Lord rises upon you
   and his glory appears over you.
3 Nations will come to your light,
   and kings to the brightness of your dawn.

When we read the story in Genesis 1, of God creating the earth, we read the words "darkness was upon the face of the deep." Physical darkness was all that existed. There was no light until God created it. After the Fall, a new type of darkness came into the world; sin grew in the human heart. Greed, selfishness, hatred, and fear spread its dark shadow over the human race. With every passing century, the black emptiness spread further and deeper. Another kind of light was needed, the light of forgiveness. Darkness of the soul is far worse than the physical darkness of the earth.

It would take more than speaking light into existence to expel the darkness of the soul of man. It would take a perfect sacrifice, a full payment of the sin committed against the Creator of all. God knew there were people on earth who loved Him and would do anything He asked of them, but there was no one who was perfect. Not a single human born could meet the specifications of the sacrificial lamb.

Stop and think a moment about how God creates each of us with a longing for Him. Many people do not recognize what this longing is; they think it is an "emptiness" created by not having enough stuff or by not being loved. Many do not know that God created them with a puzzle piece missing, and the only thing that will fill it is God. I like to call this the "God-shaped hole in our soul." Something most of us do not think about very often is the other side of the equation, that is, how God longs for us. That longing, for a relationship with us, is the entire basis of Christianity. It is the reason for Jesus coming to earth. The King of Glory gave up His majesty and honor to become one of us.

Jesus is not just another revered leader or teacher; He is the sacrificial Lamb, Who died for our sins. Without Him, we are all lost. It does not matter how good we are; we are not good enough to be reunited with our Maker. That is who Jesus is - our Mediator and the Savior of our souls.

Throughout my life, I have learned that God uses some of the most unusual people to fulfill His greatest plans. We have learned how He used a young widow woman to become the beginning of the earthly lineage of Christ. He chose a shepherd boy to bring down a giant Philistine, and He called that same young man, "a man after His own heart."

When God looks down on the sea of humanity, He does not just see a mass of people, who are all alike; He sees the heart of each individual. He loves each individual, and if they will submit to His plan for their lives, He will come and save them, setting them free forever.

Most of you have probably read or heard the story of how the Lord sent the angel Gabriel to visit a young woman, who lived in the small town of Nazareth in Galilee. Many Bible scholars agree, this young woman, Mary, was no older than sixteen years old at this time. Some of my friends reading this story may actually be older than this. I want you to read this account out of your Bible, and while you read, ponder the words; do not let complacency settle in because of the familiarity of the story. Soak each word in, and marvel at the wonder of how God chose an unlikely heroine...

 Read Luke 1: 26 - 38 - the story of the angel Gabriel's visit.

 Read Luke 1: 39 - 56 - the story of Mary's visit to her cousin Elizabeth's house

Narration Break: Retell and marvel at the miracles of our God!

We learned in our last chapter that Herod was the governor of Israel before and during the birth of Christ. He had been placed there by Augustus Caesar, who, you will remember from two chapters ago, was the nephew/adopted son of Julius Caesar. Augustus Caesar was a mighty ruler, and he kept the peace throughout his vast empire. Even though Augustus did not want anyone to call him Emperor, he truly was the first emperor of Rome.

The Roman Senate gave him the name "First Citizen," which, in Latin, is "Princeps." This is the Latin word from which we derive our English word, "prince." There were also two months on the calendar named

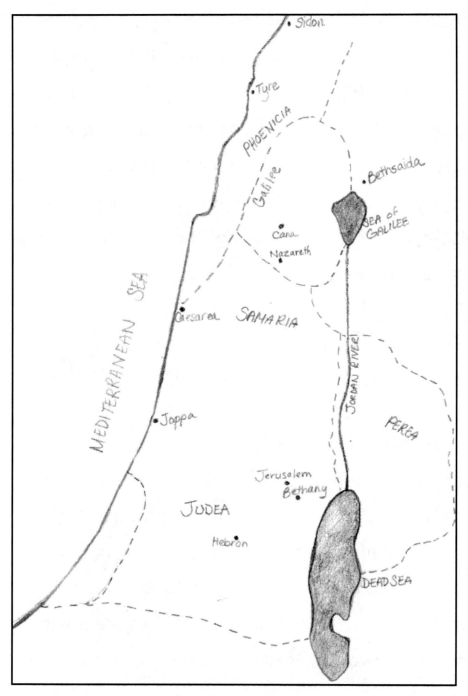

after Augustus and his adopted father, Julius. We still use these names: July and August.

Nobody ever questioned him, so Augustus made all of the rules and enforced peacekeeping techniques. As a result, citizens across the Roman Empire enjoyed safety in travel and in everyday life. Augustus also liked to know how many people were in his empire, so he ordered that a census be taken. Everyone was to return to the town of their birth and register their names where their ancestors had lived.

Chapter 24

Since both Joseph and Mary were from the house and line of David, they had to return to Bethlehem. By this time, Mary was uncomfortably large because she was nearing the end of her pregnancy. We are all familiar with this story because many of us read it, at least once a year, at Christmastime. Again, please guard against complacency and familiarity with the passage.

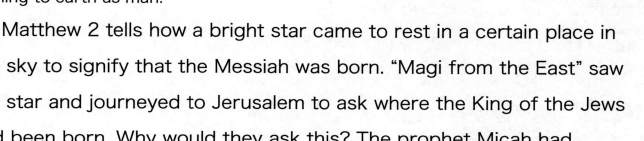 Read Luke 2 : 1 - 40, and soak in the glorious details of God coming to earth as man.

Matthew 2 tells how a bright star came to rest in a certain place in the sky to signify that the Messiah was born. "Magi from the East" saw the star and journeyed to Jerusalem to ask where the King of the Jews had been born. Why would they ask this? The prophet Micah had prophesied that out of Bethlehem would come a ruler, who would be the shepherd of God's people. The Magi had read this prophecy and had come to worship this new King.

Of course, King Herod was extremely upset by this. He told the men to go and find the child, and when they had succeeded, they were to come back and tell him, so that he, too, could go worship the child. An angel appeared to them in a dream to warn them not to go back to Herod, so they returned to their country by a different route. An angel also appeared to Joseph and told him to take the child and Mary and go to Egypt. King Herod had realized the Magi had outwitted him, and he was furious. He ordered that all little boys, two years and younger, be killed. It was this terrible incident that Jeremiah had prophesied about...

¹⁵Thus saith the LORD; A voice was heard in Ramah, lamentation, and bitter weeping; Rachel weeping for her children refused to be comforted for her children, because they were not." Jeremiah 31:15

So Jesus and his parents stayed in Egypt until the death of Herod. When Joseph and Mary returned, they moved to the town of Nazareth, and there they settled and raised their family. I have often wondered if Jesus knew right from the start that He was the Son of God. When I was a little girl, I would read the story of His birth, and then I would lie awake at night, wondering if He had the memory of being in Heaven with His Father or if the realization grew in Him as He grew older. The last part of Luke 2 tells the story of how Jesus stayed in Jerusalem and worried His parents. They found Him in the temple listening to the teachers of the Law. The Scripture tells us that Jesus told them that He was "about His Father's business."

I love the verse that says "Jesus obeyed His parents and grew in stature, in favor with both God and man." Isn't that wonderful? Jesus went through all of the same changes growing up as we all do. He was tempted in all the same ways we are, so He knows how it feels.

As we bring our chapter to a close, I would like to end with a wonderful chapter from Isaiah. God had made a plan for redemption, and as is true with all of His plans, they always come to fruition. He was going to make it possible for all people to come to Him through forgiveness. Before Jesus came, God's people, the descendants of Abraham, had a covenant with Him. Through the blood of animals, sacrificed on the altar, forgiveness was offered to those who sought it. Through Jesus, even the "Gentiles," or non-Jewish people, could be part of God's family. Read the words of Isaiah in Chapter 61. Take the time to read it out loud, and think about what it means.

Narration Break: talk about and rejoice over the most wonderful of all miracles.

"Follow Me"

The Gospel of John begins with the words, "In the beginning was the Word, and the Word was with God, and the Word was God." These words, which were inspired by the Holy Spirit, flowed onto the page from the heart of John, the Beloved Disciple. In this chapter, we are going to explore the ministry of Christ while He was here on earth as a human. In our last chapter, we learned that Jesus respected and obeyed His earthly parents, and that He grew in stature and in favor with both God and man. Jesus worked with His earthly father, Joseph, and He learned the trade of a carpenter until He was thirty years old.

During this time, Jesus's cousin, John the Baptist, was preaching and admonishing the Jews to prepare for the Lord's coming. John Chapter 1:19 says that the priests and Levites came to ask him who he was. John answered them that he was not the Christ, he was not Elijah - back from the dead, and he was not a prophet. When they demanded that John tell them who he was, so they could give an answer to those who sent them, John replied, "I am the voice of one calling in the wilderness, 'Make straight the way for the Lord.'" John baptized with water and said to the crowd, "There will be One coming after me, Whose sandals I am not worthy to unfasten."

Soon after this, Jesus came to be baptized by John...

29 The next day John saw Jesus coming toward him and said, "Look, the Lamb of God, who takes away the sin of the world! 30 This is the one I meant when I said, 'A man who comes after me has surpassed me because he was before me.' 31 I myself did not know him, but the reason I came baptizing with water was that he might be revealed to Israel." 32 Then John gave this testimony: "I saw the Spirit come down from heaven as a dove and remain on him. 33 And I

myself did not know him, but the one who sent me to baptize with water told me, 'The man on whom you see the Spirit come down and remain is the one who will baptize with the Holy Spirit.' 34 I have seen and I testify that this is God's Chosen One." [a]

35 The next day John was there again with two of his disciples. 36 When he saw Jesus passing by, he said, "Look, the Lamb of God!"" John 1:29-36

After His water baptism, Jesus asked a group of men to follow Him. These men were of various ages and from various occupations, but they all had something in common - they had to trust Jesus was who He said He was. So who were these twelve men, and why did they drop everything they were doing to follow Jesus? What made them follow this Jesus of Nazareth for three years? Could it be that God made it real to them, so they had no doubt in their minds that this, indeed, was the Messiah?

There are several passages listing the twelve disciples of Jesus. Many men in those days went by several names, so it is important to understand who exactly each one is. In John 1:35-42, the Beloved Disciple, John, explains that Andrew was standing near John the Baptist and heard him say something profound about Jesus. Read those two verses. What did John the Baptist say about Jesus?

When Andrew heard John the Baptist say this, he ran to tell his brother Simon about Jesus. Simon, who Jesus called Cephas (Peter), came and followed Jesus also. This was no coincidence. I believe these men had been chosen by God to be part of the fulfillment of the ministry of Christ here on earth. Let's learn a little more about each of the disciples. We will learn even more about many of these men, and their love for Christ, in our chapter about the first missionaries.

Andrew, brother of Peter and son of a man named Jonas, was the first to hear John the Baptist proclaim that Jesus was the Lamb of God that came to take the sin of the world. He was originally a disciple of John the Baptist because he was actively seeking to know God. Andrew is the one who brought people to Jesus; he had a servant's heart.

🌑 Luke 3 (The baptism of Jesus)

Narration Break: retell what we have learned so far.

Peter, Andrew's older brother, was a fisherman who lived in Bethsaida and Capernaum. At the time of Christ, the most common language was Greek, which was brought from the Roman Empire, but the most common family language among the Jews was Hebrew. This is why we see so many different names in the Bible for the same people. In Peter's case, his Greek name was Simon which means "rock," and his Arabic name was Cephas, which also means "rock." Peter was undeniably the leader amongst the disciples.

James (the Elder) was the older brother of John and son of Zebedee. He was a fisherman who lived in Bethsaida, and Jerusalem. We can safely assume that James and John were close brothers because they are always mentioned together in the Bible.

John, the Beloved Disciple, the younger brother of James, and young son of Zebedee, was also a fisherman by trade. Many Biblical historians believe that John was still a teenager when Jesus called him to discipleship. John followed Jesus with the kind of joyful abandonment that stirs my heart. He loved Jesus with everything he had, and Jesus loved him, too. We can thank John for the Books of John, 1st, 2nd, and 3rd John, and Revelation.

Bartholomew Nathanael is believed to be the only disciple who came from royal blood. He was a descendent of the house of Talmai, whose daughter was the wife of David and mother of Absolom. The Bible calls this disciple by his first name or his last name, and Jesus called him "An Israelite in whom there is no guile."

Matthew, also called Levi, was a tax collector. In the days of the Roman occupation, Jews detested the tax collectors because they worked for the Roman government, and most of them were greedy and dishonest. Jesus saw Matthew's heart, though, and called him to leave his money table to follow Him. Matthew wrote the book that bears his name, the first book in the New Testament.

Philip came from Bethsaida, and is thought to have been a fisherman like Peter, Andrew, James, and John. When Jesus said, "Follow Me," Philip did and gave his life to living for Jesus.

Thomas, also known by his Greek name, Didymus, lived in Galilee. Thomas is the disciple who demanded to see the risen Jesus before he believed the resurrection was true. Although Thomas was somewhat skeptical and pessimistic, he served the Lord with all of his heart, and Christ used him mightily.

James, the younger, was one of the little-known disciples. He is believed to be either the brother of the Apostle Jude or the brother of

Matthew. Jude, who also was called by the names Judas the Zealot, Thaddeus, and Lebbeus, was also a little-known disciple who came from Galilee. This man is mentioned in Luke 6:16 and Acts 1:13.

Simon the Zealot is also a disciple of whom little is known. The Bible says that he lived in Galilee, but it does not say much else. We do know that he was a "Zealot," which means he was part of a Jewish Nationalist party who hated the Roman occupation of Israel. We also see through the scripture that he laid aside his hatred and followed Jesus, adopting His message of hope and love.

Lastly, we have Judas Iscariot, the traitor who turned against Jesus in the end. Biblical historians believe that Judas was also part of the Jewish Nationalists party, but unlike Simon, Judas harbored ulterior motives for following Christ. Perhaps he secretly hoped Jesus would be the Jewish leader who would rise up and lead the Hebrews in overthrowing the Roman occupation, and when he realized this was not the purpose of Christ's ministry, he turned traitor. These are the men who walked the earth with Jesus. In our next chapter, we will read important Scripture segments about the ministry of Christ.

Narration Break: discuss the twelve disciples of Jesus.

The Miracle of Christ

"And without faith it is impossible to please God, because anyone who comes to him must believe that he exists and that he rewards those who earnestly seek him." Hebrews 11:6

Jesus, the One and only Son of God, was with God in the beginning when the world and time were created, and here He was, walking the very earth He helped create. When He stretched out His hand to heal the sick and lame, when He touched the face of a child, when He washed the feet of His disciples, His hands were once again touching the creation of His Father. None of us can imagine the depth of love which flowed from His heart. Human minds cannot fathom what it took for Him to sacrifice Himself in this way.

This is where history and the Bible collide. We tend to think of history as the happenings of humans down through the centuries, but I challenge you to think differently. I challenge you to think of history as the work of God through the ages, documented in the Bible. Jesus, God's One and only Son, came to earth as a human.

There are many indisputable accounts of the life, death, and resurrection of Jesus Christ. What other religion can say that? What other god has offered himself as an offering of atonement for the sins of mankind? What other king would lay down his crown to live the life of

his people?

Jesus started his ministry at the age of thirty, and it only lasted for three years, but during these three years, Jesus said and did more than we could ever study. Matthew, Mark, Luke, and John filled their Books of the Bible with accounts of the ministry of Jesus. As I study the words of these stories, my heart aches at the pure beauty of the life of Jesus, and I wish I could find words to express what His love does to me. I am so thankful that He knows what my heart says to His, and I pray that He enlighten each of your hearts as you read about His most precious Gift to us.

Instead of trying to capture the words and works of Jesus in my own writing, we will read the words of the apostles. Please read each of the following assigned readings carefully and remember that the words of the Scripture were Spirit breathed. If you are reading these with younger children, you may enjoy reading it from a trusted Bible story book, such as Egermeier's.

- Luke 4: 1- 13 (Satan tempts Jesus)
- Luke 6: 17- 49 (Important teachings of Jesus)

Narration Break: read and enjoy the story of Christ.

- John 6 - 11 (Accounts of Jesus's healing and teaching)
- Matthew 5 (The Beatitudes and other teachings)

Jesus knew He was going to die. He knew that He was going to have to suffer for every sin ever committed by mankind. He could have walked away from it and decided that we were not worth it, but He did not. Instead, He did His Father's will. The Son of God allowed soldiers to nail Him to that cross. The excruciating pain He had endured as they beat Him and pushed a crown of thorns into His head, paled in comparison to the completely foreign pain of bearing sin on His perfect shoulders. The perfect, spotless Lamb of God was laden with the guilt of every sin in the history of mankind. The happenings of that day are enough to make me shiver.

Matthew 27:50-53 gives some details about what happened. It says when Jesus cried out and gave up the ghost (meaning that He died), the veil of the temple was torn in half, from top to bottom. This is amazing, because it is said that the thickness of the temple veil was four inches. This passage also says the sky became dark, the earth quaked, and many of bodies of the saints, who had died, rose from the dead. Read the account of Christ's death and resurrection.

Matthew 26 - 28 (Jesus's death and resurrection)

Why would the Son of the Most High God give His life willingly for mankind? Romans 3:23 says all have sinned and have fallen short of the glory of God, and chapter 5:8 says that God demonstrates His love for us by sending Christ to die for us while we were sinners. Love. That is why Jesus died for us. This is world history at its best.

I would like to challenge each reader of this story to take personally what Jesus did. There are no human words to express what Jesus accomplished through His death and resurrection. He not only became the bridge, which spans the chasm that sin creates between the Father and us, but He conquered death. Because of His death and resurrection, those who ask for forgiveness through Him, will live with the Father in Heaven forever. For this alone, I will serve Him all of my days. However, He did not stop there! When Jesus came back from the dead, He appeared to His disciples and promised that He would send the Holy Spirit to guide and comfort His followers. We can live in victory and freedom right here on this earth. What joy! If you know this hymn, sing it together and share what Jesus means to you

Narration Break: retell the story of Jesus's life and death.

"The Old Rugged Cross" by George Bennard

1. On a hill far away stood an old rugged cross,
    The emblem of suff'ring and shame;
    And I love that old cross where the dearest and best
    For a world of lost sinners was slain.
    - o Refrain:
         So I'll cherish the old rugged cross,
         Till my trophies at last I lay down;
         I will cling to the old rugged cross,
         And exchange it some day for a crown.
2. Oh, that old rugged cross, so despised by the world,
    Has a wondrous attraction for me;
    For the dear Lamb of God left His glory above
    To bear it to dark Calvary.
3. In that old rugged cross, stained with blood so divine,
    A wondrous beauty I see,
    For 'twas on that old cross Jesus suffered and died,
    To pardon and sanctify me.
4. To the old rugged cross I will ever be true;
    Its shame and reproach gladly bear;
    Then He'll call me some day to my home far away,
    Where His glory forever I'll share.

The Roman Emperors After Christ

Some stories I have heard about the death of Christ say the Romans put Jesus to death, because they were afraid of Him. In truth, even when Jesus was trapped in a human body, He still had all dominion over the forces which were against Him. It was not the spikes driven through His hands and feet that held Him to that cross; it was the Father's love and His love for us. The Romans and the Jews, who hated Jesus, were only part of the plan. It was the plan of redemption which made Him stay His course through the pain and the mocking. It was for the Romans, as well as the rest of humanity, that Jesus took the beating.

We must remember the happenings and events in life are rarely what they seem to be. Our finite, human minds cannot comprehend the whole picture. We can study history, and indeed we must, but we will never know everything that has ever happened. God alone knows and understands when everything happened and for what reason. He alone knows every single person who will ever live, and He alone knows each one by name.

Our storyline has brought us to a pivotal point in history. You might imagine that we are standing at a crossroads. If we turn one way, we will continue down the path that says man is in control of his own earthly purpose, and we are here by coincidence. This is the mindset that leads nations and tribes to turn to idols made by their own hands. But, when

we turn the other way, there is
light. Jesus's death made a way
for forgiveness and a way to
return to the favor of our
Maker. This way says there is
hope, and there is a reason we
are all here. If you choose to
walk this way, there will be hard
times, but the separation from

God is over. Since Christ's death and resurrection, humans have had to
make the choice of which path they are going to take.

After Christ's crucifixion and resurrection, there was much unrest
between the Jews and the Romans. The Jews were tired of the high
taxes, demanded by Caesar and the foreign soldiers, who were
constantly standing guard around their cities. They wanted the power
over their own country, and little by little, the Jews started standing up
against the Romans. People in Judea even set the local Roman ruler's
house on fire. Soon, the news of these disturbances reached the ears of
Caesar, who sent more troops to squelch the rebellions.

Caesar commanded the Temple to be burned. The gold and silver
serving pieces were destroyed and melted until they ran into the cracks
between the rocks. The Temple was brought to further devastation

when the Roman soldiers dug up the foundation in order to reach the melted silver and gold.

Israel had once again been brought to desolation. Caesar did not stop here, however; he also drove the Jews out of their country, until they were scattered abroad. Now, they did not have homes, a temple, or even a country to call their own. It would be over a thousand years until their descendants were allowed to return.

Augustus Caesar had been well-loved by the Roman citizens because he took care of them and kept the peace. After the death of Caesar, the Romans were subjected to a procession of bad rulers. They did not treat the people kindly or fairly, and they raised taxes. As a result, the Roman people became poor, and the rulers became extremely wealthy.

At this time in history, the followers of Christ had earned a new name, Christians. The plan to silence the teachings of Jesus had failed. The Church had been born, and despite persecution, it would grow and spread throughout the world. In the next part of our chapter, we will hear the story of the worst Roman emperor of all; this man hated and persecuted the Roman Christians.

Narration Break: discuss what has been learned today.

The Roman Empire had quite an assortment of bad leaders and rulers, but there is one who went down in history as the very worst. This evil emperor's name was Nero. Most historians agree, Nero was mentally ill, evil, and narcissistic. No one liked him, and everyone knew that he was capable of cruel punishment, almost beyond what anyone could imagine. Nero imagined himself a great musician and spent hours playing (quite terribly) on the lyre. Everyone pretended that they thought he was a great musician, so he would not punish them.

One time, Nero left Rome for a vacation in his country home. He, and some of his family members and acquaintances, had a grand party for many days. During this time, a fire had spread and was burning the city of Rome. Even though a messenger came to tell the emperor that Rome was burning, Nero did not come back. Instead he sent the messenger away, after scolding him for interrupting the party. By the time Nero finally returned to Rome, there was wide-spread destruction throughout the city. Many families were without homes, and everyone was angry at Nero for staying away.

Nero wanted to take the attention off of himself, so he blamed a group of people who annoyed him. He told the citizens of Rome that the Christians were the ones to blame for setting the fire and that they should be punished for it. Some people believed him, and soon, hatred for the Christians started to grow. The evil in Nero was threatened by Jesus in the Christians, and soon they became his target for hatred. I will not go into details of how the early Christians were persecuted by Nero; the details are gruesome and enough to make one sick. It is enough to say that the many recorded details of this time outline this fact: many Christians lost their lives at the hands of Nero.

Soon, there was such animosity toward the Christians, they decided to make secret places for their meetings. They dug passage- ways, called catacombs, under the city of Rome. Archaeologists have discovered many of the catacombs, along with graves where the early Christians buried their dead. The Christians also made a code to talk to each other. They had signs to show that they were Christians and it was

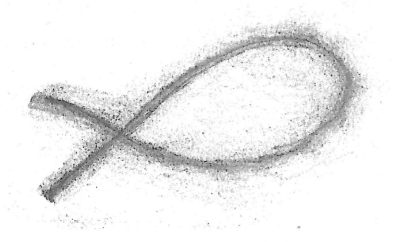

safe to talk about Jesus. The fish symbol, which we often see as a decorative car decal, is one of these signs.

In our next chapter, we will study the first Christian

missionaries. I find this time period absolutely fascinating. Christianity was like a young plant, which had germinated at the death and resurrection of our Lord Jesus Christ. The hope, which comes from promises fulfilled, had taken root deep in the hearts and souls of those who were searching. Even though there was great evil that threatened to stomp out Christianity while it was still a tender shoot, God used the persecution to scatter His followers into various locations around the world. It is true that our faith grows stronger through times of trouble, and we see that this was true then as well, for even when Nero persecuted them, the Christian church grew and spread. In this way, Christianity spread quickly.

After Nero died, other emperors continued to persecute the Christians, but none of them were quite as evil as Nero. Sometime after Nero's reign, an emperor, named Constantine, came to the throne. Constantine was a fair ruler and was known for being kind to the Christians. At first, Constantine worshipped other gods, but then something happened - he became a Christian! How did this happen? Some say Constantine was preparing to lead his men into a battle. The night before the battle was to happen, he had a dream about the cross of Christ. When he awoke, he told his men that they must fight in the name of the God of the Christians. Constantine and his army won the battle, and the emperor became a believer. Many of Constantine's people came to believe in God also.

Rome had always been the capitol of the Roman Empire, but Constantine decided to make Constantinople the new capitol city. Under Constantine's rule, the Roman Empire had peace, and the Christians had a reprieve from the persecution which had been inflicted upon them for so many years. Peace, prosperity, and power were not to last for long; however, the Roman Empire was in its last days as the super power of the earth.

Narration Break: retell the stories of Nero and Constantine.

The End of the Road

Parent Note: please pre-read the first section of this chapter before reading it to small children.

Well, here we are, at the end of our journey together. The study of history is such a wonderful journey, and I have enjoyed every step of this one. I pray that your heart has been drawn to the heart of the Father, as we have studied together.

In our last few chapters, we have learned a little about Jesus's disciples and the early Church, which formed after His death and resurrection. Even while enduring unspeakable persecution, the Church grew and blossomed. The hope of Jesus grew in the hearts of these new believers and became a light in the darkness of sin and hopelessness.

One of my favorite stories of early missionary work is the story of Saul turned Paul. Saul had been raised in a traditional Jewish home, steeped in the law and educated in the ways of the Old Testament Jews. The laws, which God had given in Exodus and Leviticus, were what Saul lived for. While Jesus walked the earth as a human, Saul did not know him. As Jesus hung on the cross, Saul was completely unaware of how his future was going to be absolutely opposite of anything he could have ever imagined. Jesus has a way of doing that!

The growing number of Christians agitated the legalistic Jews. Even though they all knew His coming had been promised, they held the law as their god and were not ready to let it go to be replaced by the promise fulfilled. Jesus called these people "white-washed sepulchers" in Matthew 23 - white on the outside and full of the dead on the inside. Saul was among these men. He loved the law and hated this Jesus, who people believed to be the Messiah.

Saul's hatred for the Christians became a fuel, which burned in his soul. He sought them out and persecuted them harshly. It was Saul who was present at the stoning of Stephen, the first martyr for Christ. It was he who nodded his head in permission for the first stone to be thrown. Read Acts 7 - 8:3 for the account of the questioning and death of Stephen.

However, God had plans for this man, Saul, with the stone cold heart. On one of his trips to persecute the Christians, Saul met up with the One he was persecuting. A blinding light came, and Saul fell to the ground. Saul became Paul that day, and the persecutor became as one he had persecuted. What an amazing story of God's power and forgiveness! Paul went on to become the first missionary to the Gentile world. The man, who had hated Christians, became one of the most avid followers of Christ. Paul wrote a whole section of books in the Bible, including Romans, 1 and 2 Corinthians, Galatians, Ephesians, Philippians, Colossians, 1 and 2 Thessalonians, 1 and 2 Timothy, Titus, and Philemon. What power comes from the broken and forgiven!

Also among the first missionaries, were many of the twelve Apostles of Christ. Most of them became martyrs for their faith. Andrew ministered in Scythia, Greece, and Asia Minor, and was killed in Patra, Greece, when he was crucified on an X-shaped cross. Bartholomew was a missionary in Armenia. He died the death of a martyr in India. James, the elder brother of John, preached in Jerusalem and Judea, and it was here that he, too, died as a martyr. James, the younger, preached in Palestine and Egypt, and he also died as a martyr in Egypt.

John, the Beloved Disciple, preached among the churches of Asia Minor and, unlike the other disciples, died of natural causes. Jude, preached in Assyria and Persia. He died as a martyr in Persia. Matthew ministered in Ethiopia and also died a martyr's death there. Peter did his missionary work among the Jews, going as far as Babylon. His death is recorded as a martyr's death, when he was crucified upside down. He did not think himself worthy to die in the upright manner that Jesus had suffered. Philip preached and died as a martyr in Hierapolis.

Simon, the Zealot, ministered to his fellow Jews and was martyred. Thomas fulfilled his missionary calling in Parthia, Persia, and India. He died as a martyr in India. You many have guessed by now, that it was dangerous to be a Christian at this time in history, but the followers of Jesus took seriously the call to spread the hope of Jesus's forgiveness. Before He returned to Heaven, Jesus said...

"Go ye therefore, and teach all nations, baptizing them in the name of the Father, and of the Son, and of the Holy Ghost. Teaching them to observe all things whatsoever I have commanded you: and, lo, I am with you alway, even unto the end of the world. Amen." Matthew 28:19-20

Narration Break: talk about what we have learned so far.

In our last chapter, we learned about some of the Roman emperors who lived after Christ. One of them, Nero, was an extremely evil man who persecuted the Christians. When Julius Caesar and Augustus Caesar were rulers, Rome was strong, However, the procession of weak or selfish emperors, who ruled after them, weakened Rome. The empire was so large, there was no way to protect it all or to make sure that everyone everywhere had what they needed.

It was around this time that the Celts, who lived to the north in Britain, became a problem to the Roman Empire. The Celts had never completely fallen to the Roman Empire, and still had large areas that were not under Roman control. The Celts rose up together and drove the Romans completely out of Britain. The Roman Empire was loosing some of its outer-lying provinces, which did nothing to help with the weakening borders.

Finally, an emperor came along who was wise enough to see this. This emperor, Diocletian (DIE-o-KLEE-shun), decided to split the empire into two sections and appoint another emperor to help rule the western portion, while he ruled the eastern portion. In theory this should have have worked well, as long as there were two emperors who were not trying to fight each other to become the head ruler of the empire again, and for awhile, it did work. Eventually, the western part of the empire became weaker and more susceptible to foreign attack, while the eastern part became stronger and richer.

There came a time when western Rome could not defend itself against the raiding barbarians who were pounding their borders. The most fearsome of the barbarians were the Huns. These people wore strange, rough clothes and ate foods that were considered inedible. The Huns were considered to be uncouth and rude, uncivilized and uneducated. Even their war horses were tough! The Huns terrorized everyone in their path, including the weakened western Roman citizens.

The most infamous of the Huns was Attila. This barbarian leader was the most feared of all Huns. He attempted to conquer the Western and

Eastern Roman Empire; however, he was unable to take the Eastern Empire's capital city of Constantinople. Attila also set his mind on taking Roman Gaul (which is now France). In the year AD 451, he crossed the Rhine River, but he was defeated at Aurelianum. Next he invaded Italy and rampaged through their northern provinces. Attila died in AD 453, before he could fulfill his dream of taking Rome.

The Huns were not the only Barbarians the Romans dealt with; there were also the Visigoths. They were one of the two main branches of the Goths, a large, roving band of barbarians. (The other branch was the Ostrogoths.) The Visigoths settled around the Danube River with the permission of the Roman emperor. Soon, however, the relationship soured, and the Visigoths became intent on the destruction of the Roman Empire. In AD 376, a six-year revolt broke out, and there was much plundering and devastation in the Balkans.

The end of the Roman Empire had come. The split, which had been meant to strengthen the empire, eventually caused their demise instead. The Western Roman Empire was destroyed by the barbarians when the Eastern Empire did not help them fight the barbarians. The Eastern Empire was not even called Rome anymore, it was called the Byzantine Empire. We will learn more about this empire in our next volume of history.

Many people say the Roman Empire did not really fall. Rather, they say, it diversified; parts of it became the roots of other nations and empires. I do find it rather interesting that the word Caesar lives on in different languages. For example, rulers in Russia were once called "Czars," which translated, means Caesar.

The "iron leg" kingdom had come to an end. What is next on your "Dream Statue?" The iron and clay mixed feet are the last section you will be adding to your statue project. What is the "iron/clay feet" kingdom? Some say that it has something to do with the Roman Catholic Church, while others point to the Islamic Empire. I am not going to speculate on the interpretation of this last kingdom, because I do not feel it is within my bounds. If the Bible does not state clearly, than we will leave it at that.

We do know, however, there is another Kingdom coming, don't we? What was it that came and hit the statue at the feet, completely destroying the entire thing? It was a Rock, not cut by human hand, that came and set up a Kingdom on the earth. Jesus told His disciples that He would be returning to earth, and He is called the Rock, the Cornerstone, in many places in the Bible. He was not destroyed by human hands, merely sacrificed to fulfill His Father's plan of redemption. He will be back, and I cannot wait for that day!

Narration Break: Celebrate the end of the journey through the Story of the Ancients! Read the last "Apologetics through Archaeology" section.

John 14... Read the words of comfort from our Savior and rejoice!

Appendix Title Page

- Apologetics through Archaeology Section
- Deeper Research Topics
- Optional Lesson Plan
- Optional Crafts and Projects
- Optional Book Lists
- Works cited

What worldview glasses do you wear?

Apologetics through Archaeology

Know how to defend your faith with science and history. The theory of evolution has attacked our Christian faith for too many years. As Christians, we need to know, beyond a shadow of doubt, that we have REAL science on our side.

Romans 1:20 "For the invisible things of Him from the creation of the world are clearly seen, being understood by the things that are made, even His eternal power and Godhead; so that they are without excuse."

This means that God made the earth and all of creation to be a visible show of His existence. When we see a beautiful house, we don't say, "Wow! That is an amazing house! I wonder how it came into being? There must have been an explosion at the lumber yard, and this majestic estate is the result of that accident!" No, we know if there is a house there, then someone MADE it. The same is true with creation. If there is a creation, and clearly there is, then there is a Creator. God is the Creator. He gave us creation as a visible sign of Himself, He sent Jesus as a flesh and blood person Who was documented in history, and He gave us the Bible - the very Word of God.

Please note: there will not be an "Apologetics through Archaeology" section for every chapter. Most sections line up with the topic of the chapter being read, while others are "random," interesting facts that do not go perfectly with the chapter topic.

● **#1** What exactly is archaeology, anyway? Many people associate archaeology with the study of evolution and the scientists working to prove that theory, but did you know that many Christian archaeologists have discovered numerous geological finds that support the Bible? By doing this, they have moved the "stories and accounts" in the Bible from "pious tales" to the history books. The Bible gives detailed accounts of battles, locations of cities, and famous kings' riches. These Bible-believing archaeologists have yet again proven that the Bible is indeed a trustworthy source for history! For years, people of all religious standings have argued about the age of the earth. Do some research and discussion about the different theories. Discuss this question: why do some people take the time periods given in other places in the Bible as literal, twenty-four days just as we know them, but not the days spoken about in Genesis 1? When you read about the Great Flood (which we will learn about later), the Bible says that it rained 40 days and 40 nights. I have never heard anyone argue that those days might be "a thousand years." Why would the days of Creation be any different?

⬤ **#2** Have you ever been lost for words when someone demands scientific evidence that the flood is real and that it covered the earth? Here are five points of evidence to refute such an argument. (The quote in point 4 is from Answers in Genesis website. Footnote 1a.)

1. Fossils of sea creatures have been found in rock layers which cover all of the continents. The Grand Canyon, which is more than a mile above sea level, has marine fossils! Beautifully preserved fossils of sea creatures are found in many places, way above sea level, due to the ocean waters flooding over all of the continents.

2. Many fossil "graveyards" have been found that contain beautifully preserved fossils, which proves rapid burial of plant and animal species.

3. Rapid deposit has left sediment layers, which spread over huge areas of the planet. There are rock layers that are traceable across entire continents. The physical features of these layers prove the rapid deposit of tons of rock, soil, and minerals.

4. "Sediment transported long distances. We find that the sediments in those widespread, rapidly deposited rock layers had to be eroded from distant sources and carried long distances by fast-moving water. For example, the sand for Coconino Sandstone of Grand Canyon (Arizona) had to be eroded and transported from the northern portion of what is now the United States and Canada. Furthermore, water current indicators (such as ripple marks), preserved in rock layers, show that for '300 million years' water currents were consistently flowing from northeast to southwest across all of North and South America, which, of course, is only possible over weeks during a global flood." (Answers in Genesis #2)

5.Under normal circumstances, rock does not bend; they break because they are hard and brittle, but in many places all over the world, there are huge sections of whole sequences of strata that are bent without fracture lines. This would indicate that all of the rock layers were rapidly deposited and "folded" while they were still in a wet and "pliable" state.

● #3 Out of all the creatures that God Created, dinosaurs have been the most misused by evolutionists. So are there dinosaurs in the Bible? The actual word "dinosaur" was invented in 1841, but the creature was created on the sixth day along with all the other land animals. Job 40: 15 - 19 says, "Look now at the behemoth, which I made along with you; he eats grass like an ox. See now, his strength is in his hips, And his power is in his stomach muscles. He moves his tail like a cedar; the sinew of his thighs are tightly knit. His bones are like beams of bronze, his ribs like bars of iron. He is the first of the ways of God; only He who made him can bring near His sword."

Were there dinosaurs on the Ark? The Bible says that there were two of "every kind of animal and seven of some" that went into the Ark. There is a difference between species and kinds. When the Bible uses the word "kind," it is talking about families. Before the flood, there were many species of dinosaurs. If two of every kind of dinosaur went on the ark, that means there were about one hundred dinosaurs on the Ark. What happened to the dinosaurs? Why are there none today? Dr. Ken Ham, of Answers in Genesis, says this:

"At the time of the Flood, many of the sea creatures died, but some survived. In addition, all of the land creatures outside the Ark died, but the representatives of all the kinds that survived on the Ark lived in the new world after the Flood. Those land animals (including dinosaurs) found the new world to be much different than the one before the Flood. Due to (1) competition for food that was no longer in abundance, (2) other catastrophes, (3) man killing for food (and perhaps for fun), and (4) the destruction of habitats, etc., many species of animals eventually died out. The group of animals we now call dinosaurs just happened to die out too. In fact, quite a number of animals become extinct each year. Extinction seems to be the rule in Earth history (not the formation of new types of animals as you would expect from evolution)." [1b] (I highly recommend reading "Dinosaurs for Kids" written by Ken Ham.)

#4 After many years had passed, and everyone who knew how to read and write in

hieroglyphics had died, the meaning of the symbols had all been forgotten. It was not until the year 1799 that there was hope of ever being able to "crack the code" of the ancient Egyptians. It was in that year, a French soldier dug up a stone, which had strange writing and symbols engraved on it. The stone had a story or passage engraved in hieroglyphics, along with the same passage in two known languages. It took nearly twenty

years to unlock the code. Because it was found near the town of Rosetta, in the Nile Delta, the stone became known as the Rosetta Stone. You may see this famous stone someday if you visit the British Museum.

#5 Charles Darwin, the father of the theory of evolution said, "...All organic beings which have ever lived on the earth have descended from some one primordial form." This means, his theory states, that all the amazing creatures which God created in six days, were, in actuality, evolved over millions of years.

In truth, every single creature in God's creation completely debunks the entire evolution theory. You could choose any given creature, and after any amount of investigation, you would discover that the creature would have gone extinct before it could have evolved. All animals have defense mechanisms that had to be intact and complete the first time they used them. A dead animal does not reproduce and, therefore, would be irreversibly extinct.

Note of interest: Darwin did not know about DNA. National Geographic Magazine said, [the discovery of the existence of DNA] "... turns the spotlight on his biggest mistakes. Darwin's own ideas on the mechanism of inheritance were a mess - and wrong."

⬤**#6** A couple of years ago, I had the profound honor of seeing the Dead Sea Scrolls. These ancient manuscripts were found in the years 1947 and 1956, in a series of caves on the northwest shore of the Dead Sea. These scrolls are dated several hundred years before Christ through approximately one hundred years after Christ. The scrolls, which are handwritten, are copies of the Book of Psalms, Deuteronomy, Genesis, Isaiah, Exodus, Leviticus, Numbers, some of the minor Prophets, Daniel, Jeremiah, Ezekiel, Job, and 1 & 2 Samuel. As I stood in the room where the scrolls were on display, my heart was skipping with joy, for there, around me, were sections of my very favorite Books of the Bible, written in their original Hebrew and Aramaic. I learned that day, there was a tribe of Israelites, who had the job of transcribing these scrolls. From the time they were young, they were taught how to read and write skillfully, so they could carefully write copies of these God-breathed books. The tour guide at the museum explained to us that the scrolls, even though they were copies of the same book, were written by different people and at different times. For example, one of the copies of Isaiah was over one hundred years older than the other, and you could tell, by the handwriting, it was written by a different hand. As I stood there, the truth soaked into me. The Word of God will always live on.

The "holy book" of the Islamic world may contradict the Bible, but in the end, truth will always win. Recently, I had a learned friend point out to me that the Koran is the only "holy book" that blatantly says that Jesus did not die and rise from the dead. What I find somewhat puzzling is that the Koran was written after Christ by more than 600 years. The Bible had been handwritten for hundreds and hundreds of years before this, passed down from generation to generation. Historical documentation, found throughout the Middle East, agree with historical happenings in the Bible.

⬤**#7** Eighty miles south of Cairo, Egypt, in the middle of the fertile Faiyum, is a town named Medinet-el-Faiyum. This town is a beautiful, lush oasis in the middle of the desert. It is known for its oranges, peaches, olives, pomegranates, and many other fruits. What causes this oasis to be there? A manmade canal, which is over 200 miles long, conveys water of the Nile into this area, turning what otherwise would be desert into a fertile paradise. Throughout Egypt, this waterway, which dates back to ancient times, is called "Bahr Yusuf" - "Joseph's Canal." It was Pharaoh's "Grand Vizier," Joseph, who designed it and had it built!

⬤**#8** The Pharaoh, in Chapter 8, who was afraid of the Children of Israel, was of a different line of kings. The one, who was in power during (and for some time before) Joseph's being sold by his brothers, was from the days of the Hyksos. Because the Hyksos had come in and overthrown the dynasty before them, they were "cordially detested" by the Egyptians, and their reigns were not diligently recorded by the Egyptian scribes. There are also very few written records of the Pharaoh's officials. By the time Joseph had died and several hundred years had gone by, the Pharaoh who came to power, was not informed of the happenings of the Hyksos Pharaoh and his Grand Vizier. All this Pharaoh knew was that there was a large sub-nation, growing stronger and stronger right under his nose. Whether this Pharaoh was Ramesses II or one of his predecessors, he did not care how the Hebrews had gotten there; he just wanted to insure that they did not take over his country. Exodus 1:8-11 says that Pharaoh afflicted the Children of Israel with heavy burdens and the building of treasure-cities for Pithom and Ramesses. West of the city of Thebes, there is a rock tomb. Inside of this tomb are spacious vaults with rock walls. It is on one of these walls, archaeologists discovered a series of paintings from the life of an Egyptian dignitary, showing what he had accomplished for his country. One of the scenes show him in charge of public works. The scene shows, in great detail, the Hebrews working under the scrutiny of Egyptian taskmasters. In hieroglyphics, the inscription says, "The rod is in my hand. Be not idle."

●#9 It was during the hundreds of years, when the Children of Israel were in Egypt, that Hammurabi of Babylon fought and won the battles, which expanded his kingdom throughout the Fertile Crescent. The archaeological discoveries in Egypt, which are dated at the time of Hammurabi's conquest, show Egyptian apprehension. Would the great Babylonian king set his sights on Egypt as his next conquest? Even though it was a hard time for the Children of Israel, it truly was God's protection for His people. If they had been in Canaan, they would not have been strong enough to stand against Hammurabi's conquests.

●#10 Jericho, the city that so famously fell without a fight, is an object of fascination to the world of Christian archaeology. The walls, that came crashing down at the shout of the people and the blast from the trumpets, were discovered by archaeologists in the early 1900's. There have been many debates on whether or not these were the exact walls that came crashing down, or if they were the rebuilt ones. Either way, the walls of ancient Jericho were massively thick. There were two sets of walls, one inside of the other. The inside wall was twelve feet thick, while the outer one was six feet thick. Together, they created such an immense military fortification. The thought that they would tumble down by mere shouting and trumpet blowing is almost ridiculous! Only God could have brought this city down.

⬤*#11* The great civilizations of Babylon and Assyria were situated between the mighty Rivers Euphrates and Tigris. It was during Hammurabi's reign that the Assyrian nation crumbled and fell. The Assyrians were known for being fierce and rather ill-tempered. They were also known to be cruel to the peoples who they conquered.

In the ancient days, there was a well-known city named Mari located between the rivers. This city was thought to be the tenth city founded after the flood. The beauty of this city was well-known. Archaeologists and historians of modern times heard about this city through studying the writings of other civilizations and other cities located in Mesopotamia. They knew that it was a grand city, with many riches, but there was a problem; they did not know where it had been located.

One day in 1933, there was excitement in the world of archaeology; someone had found, quite by accident, an artifact that dated back to the time of Mari's heyday. After working for about six years, the entire city of Mari was uncovered. This ancient city had served as the capital city during the days of Nimrod. Ancient frescoes showed scenes of the rulers, who had held power thousands of years before. Before the very eyes of these excited archaeologists, the world, of over four thousand years ago, came to life in an unimaginable way. They could also see the ruin and rubble from the battle that ended Mari's glory days. Hammurabi had arrived with his mighty Babylonian army, and Mari came under his control. Babylon was beginning to swallow up the Fertile Crescent.

●#12 When we are reading about the Ancients, it is easy to lose track of what happened when. I love history and have studied it for a good many years, but I still have to be reminded of how many years most people lived in those days. For example, Noah lived 950 years. If we compare that to what was happening in the Americas 950 years ago, it is shocking! For example, if you were born 950 years ago, you would have been born in the year 1062. You would have already been 430 years old when Columbus sailed the ocean blue. Here is another interesting fact: Abraham was born only two years after Noah died. This means that Abraham could have easily talked to Noah's son, Shem, who actually outlived him. When you consider how long everyone lived, it is easier to understand how there came to be so many people so quickly after the flood. I once studied a chart that showed the generations between Noah and Jacob (Israel). The chart showed that there were ten generations of people living all at one time! If there were that many people living at one time, the extended families would overlap and spread out into the family tree branches until they were out of sight.

●#13 Read Numbers 13:22-33. When I first read this many years ago, I was startled to read the words "land of giants." Who were these people, and were they really giants or simply people who were bigger than the Israelites? The words , the"Children of Anak" give us a clue, because Anak means "long-necked." Historians believe that the "Children of Anak" were very tall, and large people with characteristically long necks. They are believed to be possible survivors of ancient pre-Semitics. An accidental archaeological find in 1887 sheds a little light on the kinds of people and cities the Israelites encountered when they entered Canaan. "Further investigation produced eventually a collection of 377 documents in all." ("The Bible as History" [1]) These letters, to and from the royal archives of Amenophis III and the princes of Palestine and Phoenicia, were written in Akkadian, which was the "diplomatic" language of the second millennium BC. These letters were written according to the current protocol and outlined the building of huge, fortified cities. These cities were the ones the terrified spies reported to Moses in Numbers 13:17-18 and Deuteronomy 1:28.

- - - - - - - - - - - - - - - - - - - -*Apologetics through Archaeology*- -

⚫**#14 & 15** The stories of the Judges of Israel are fascinating, but are they truly real? "The background of these 'pious tales' is made up of facts, contemporary events which as a result of recent research can be dated with considerable accuracy." During the time that the Israelites had settled their Promised Land and built their cities, there were tribes in the mountains of Galilee, which were being oppressed by the Canaanites. (Genesis 49:14-15) It was then that Deborah summoned Israel to fight for their freedom. The tribe of Issachar was being oppressed. From this tribe came a man named Barak. He joined Deborah in leading the revolt against the oppressors. Judge 5:19 says they "...fought the kings of Canaan in Taanach by the waters of Megiddo." They won this battle with the Lord's help.

Taanach and Megiddo are situated about 5 miles apart on the plain of Jezreel. At about 1450 BC, Taanach was a large and busy city-state, and Megiddo was a small, Egyptian-dominated town. Around 1150 BC, Megiddo was deserted after being destroyed. It was not rebuilt or inhabited until 1100 BC. Archaeologists have discovered pottery from these settlers. The same types of pottery have been found in other settlements, in the mountains of that region; they are Israelite pottery.

Taanach is specifically mentioned in the Song of Deborah. "The reference to its being 'by the waters of Megiddo' is presumably a more precise description of its situation. Megiddo itself, whose 'water' is the river Kishon, cannot at that time have been in existence." ("The Bible as History" [2]) These archaeological discoveries match these Biblical references. They both speak of the happenings of about 1125 BC.

⚫**#16** Where did the Midianites come from? What were their roots? Genesis 25:2-6 says they descended from Abraham's wife, Keturah. (Abraham married Keturah after Sarah died.) Also, in their ancestry, is Jethro, a priest of the Midianites who was also the father-in-law of Moses (Zeporah's father). Numbers 21:4-9 tells the story of Israel's whining and complaining and the Lord's punishment - snake bites. It tells of how Moses prayed for the people and how the Lord instructed him to make a bronze snake on a pole. This snake on the pole became an idol among the Midianites, who were with the Israelites at the time.

An archaeologist, named Benno Rothenberg, found a tabernacle dating back to this time. In the Holy of Holies, there was a small statue/idol of the snake on a pole, exactly as God had told Moses to make, and exactly as described in the Numbers 21 account. Although God did not approve of them making this snake and pole into an idol, it does verify the authenticity of the statue from God's instructions.

● **#17 & 18** After the death of the great King Solomon, the Kingdom of Israel divided. The destruction of Israel was on their own heads. Eventually, Israel would fall prey to Assyria, and Israel would be conquered by Babylon. 1 Kings 15:22 says, "... and King Asa built with them Geba of Benjamin and Mizpah." What was Mizpah? Mizpah was a massively big fortress between Judah and Israel. It seems that there was quite a lot of civil unrest between the Northern and Southern Kingdoms, and because of this, they felt they needed to ready themselves for battle.

An American archaeological expedition, from the Pacific School of Religion, which was led by Dr. William Frederick Bade, in 1927-35, excavated the remains of a staggeringly massive stonework, seven miles north of Jerusalem. It was Mizpah! With walls that spanned 26 feet in width, this fortress reveals to us just how bitter the civil war was between the split kingdoms of Israel.

Also discovered among the ruins of that time period, are the evidences, that many in Israel did evil in the sight of the Lord. As described throughout Kings, idol worship and horrible acts of (human) sacrifices were prevalent and are evident in the archaeological finds dated during that time period.

● **#19** When the Hebrews were allowed to return to Jerusalem to rebuild their city and temple, it did not happen immediately. In fact, they waited until Nehemiah became governor. He ordered the walls to be built. Nehemiah 4:17 tells us that "everyone with one of his hands wrought in the work, and with other handheld a weapon." This rebuilding of the walls was actually a fast repair job. A British archaeologist, by the name of J. Garrow Duncan, found and excavated sections of this wall. His reports said, "The stones are small, rough, irregular, and unequal. Some of them are unusually small and seem to be merely chips broken off from bigger stones. The large holes and hollow spaces are filled up with a haphazard mixture of clay and plaster mixed with tiny chips of stone..." This was the rebuilt wall of Jerusalem.

The Israelites knew Persia was their ruler. They asked King Darius II for his approval to make the Law of God, the law of Israel and Jews everywhere. The king approved. This is clearly indicated in Ezra 7:23-26. In the year 1905, three papyrus documents were discovered on the Island of Elephantine, an island which lies beside the first cataract of the Nile, near the Aswan Dam. These documents, which are dated 419 BC, are instructions on how to make the Feast of Passover a time of celebrations. The writings are signed by Hananiah, "agent for Jewish affairs at the Court of the Persian governor of Egypt." Archaeological finds, dated around this time from Israel, show that the Jews, living in the rebuilt city of Israel, did not have lives even remotely resembling that of their ancestors during the glory days of David and Solomon's reigns. They lived simple and rather poor lives. Archaeological evidence shows no big buildings were built, and no great works of art were created during this period.

●#20 Some of the most amazing and puzzling archaeological and historical discoveries on the North and South American continents are the Ica Stones. The Deeper Research this week is concerning these stones. Please find a Christian Creationist article on these interesting finds.

#21 It was during the 4th century that the political power of the ancient world shifted from the Fertile Crescent area toward the West. The silver arms and chest kingdom was fading, and the bronze stomach and thighs kingdom was about to rise. Alexander the Great defeated Darius III of Persia in 333 BC. With this victory, Alexander took the leading role of power.

On his march down to Egypt, Alexander and his army stopped twice to fight, once at Tyre, the heavily fortified Phoenician city. Tyre was built on an island and had high, protective walls all the way around it. Most generals would not have even considered attacking, but 24 year old Alexander put an offensive action plan into motion. He divided his men into three separate task forces, assigning one group the job of building a 2,000 foot "mole" out to the island city of Tyre. He assigned the second group to protect the builders of the mole from attack. Lastly, he gave the third group the job of building Helepolis. These structures were monstrous, mobile, protective towers, which were many stories high. They held the bowmen and light artillery. The towers had drawbridges on the front, which enabled a surprise attack on the enemy city's wall. The mobile attack towers, that Alexander's men built and used, were twenty stories high and at least 150 feet above the highest city wall. It took them seven months to prepare for their attack on Tyre. Zechariah 9:3-4 gives some insight about what Tyre was doing at the time. "And [Tyre] did build herself a strong hold, and heaped up silver as the dust, and fine gold as the mire of the streets. Behold the Lord will cast her out, and He will smite her power in the sea..."

Zechariah 9:5 goes on to say that "Gaza shall be very sorrowful." These commentaries in Zechariah are widely accepted as a commentary from the Jewish community of that time. After Gaza had fallen, Alexander's path to the Nile and Egypt was open.

●**#22 - 27** It was during the period of the Greek Empire that the Hebrew Scriptures were translated into Greek. Many Jews moved to various locations, including Egypt. Since Egypt was under the control of the Greek Empire, Greek influence was strong.

There were Greek kings who were very wicked. At the top of this list would be Antiochus IV, called Epiphanies. He defiled the temple, destroying and plundering the city of Jerusalem. He and his men took the women and children captive. The worship of Olympian god Zeus was set up in the Temple of Yahweh. By the time of Christ, the Jewish people had become saturated with Greek cultural influences. They were under the control of Rome, but Rome was also heavily influenced by the Greeks. The cities of Palestine were of Greek influence. Only the small towns and villages had managed to hold onto their traditional Jewish flavor. This was the "Israel" that Jesus was born into.

The Old Testament covers thousands of years, while the New Testament gives account of less than 100 years. The archaeological-Biblical records end around the time of Christ, as history steps from the "Ancient/Biblical" era to the next time period. Archaeologists have uncovered the ruins of many Roman conquests throughout what we call Palestine and Syria. After Caesar completely destroyed the temple and disbanded the Jews, they wandered and resettled in lands around the globe.

Deeper Research Topics for Older Students

Look at the BIG picture....

On the following pages, you will find deeper research topics for your older students. There are topics for each chapter, which are divided into junior high and senior high school levels.

※ The junior high topics are marked with this bullet point mark.

⬤ The senior high topics are marked with this bullet point mark.

(Some of these assignments would best be accomplished by reading the chapter in its entirety.)

Deeper Research Topics for Older Students

Chapter 1

✱ Using Genesis chapters 4 and 5, create a family tree or timeline for the family of Adam and Eve.

⬤ Do some research on the theory of evolution. Compare it to the Genesis account of creation. Write a report about the differences. If you know how to write a compare and contrast essay, do so with this topic as your subject. (Suggestion: because evolution is such a wide topic, you will want to narrow your topic down to one or two points of interest. For example: How does evolution explain away the fact that humans have thoughts and language, and animals do not?)

Chapter 2

✱ Research different opinions about how long it took to build the ark. Which one do you most agree with? Why?

⬤ Some geologists think that the flood was not truly a global flood. The Bible states that God sent water to cover the face of the earth. What do you think? Do you think that the flood, indeed, covered the face of the entire earth, or do you agree with the geologists who think that it covered the "known world" of that time? (Suggestion: do some research on the fossil records gathered by Creationists scientist. What do these records tell us about a global flood versus a more "local" flood?)

Chapter 3

✱ Research the farming techniques of the Ancient Egyptians. Write a paragraph for each technique you find and draw a picture illustrating how they worked.

⬤ The Nile River is the longest river in the world. It is abundant in wildlife and vegetation. Do some research on the Nile River. Draw a map and write at least one page about what you find.

Deeper Research Topics for Older Students

Chapter 4

✻ Ancient Egyptians are not the only civilization that mummified their dead. Do some research about other civilizations that used this method of preserving their dead. Write the information you find.

⬤ There were many Ancient Egyptian tombs that were robbed over the centuries. In 1922, there was a buzz of excitement in the world of archaeology. A beautifully preserved and completely in tact tomb had been discovered! "King Tut," as he would become known, was a young Pharaoh who died from mysterious causes. <u>This is the topic of your first quarter research project. From now, till the end of the first quarter (5 weeks from now), take your time to do a large research project.</u> This week, decide how you are going to display your information, and start your research. Some display suggestions are: 1.) use a large, cardboard fold out to artfully display pictures and your written (or typed and printed) information, 2.) write a traditional report and place it in a three-prong folder along with any printed or drawn illustrations, 3.) make a <u>large</u> lap-book by joining three, large file folders - place all of your information in the lapbook. (A lapbook can be compared to a large, cardboard fold out, just on a smaller scale.)

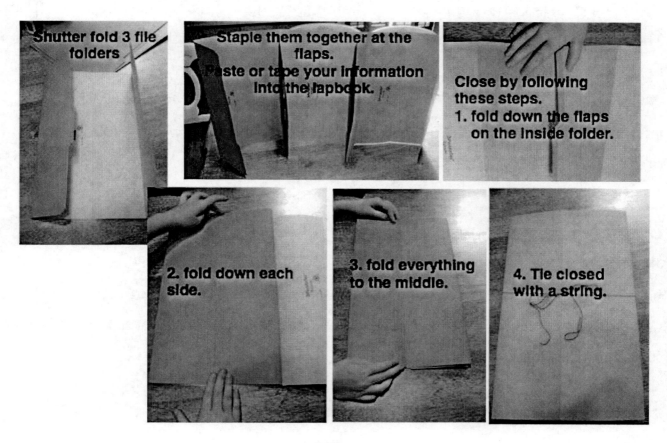

Shutter fold 3 file folders

Staple them together at the flaps.
Paste or tape your information into the lapbook.

Close by following these steps.
1. fold down the flaps on the inside folder.

2. fold down each side.

3. fold everything to the middle.

4. Tie closed with a string.

Deeper Research Topics for Older Students

Chapter 5

✱ After studying the map in your Chapter 5 Journal pages, research and record what modern day countries are now located in the area of Abraham's travels.

● Continue to work on your report. This week, read at least 5 sources; one a day would be good way to plan. (Remember as you take notes, also write down the name of the resource and the author. You will need this information for your bibliography page.)

Chapter 6

✱ In this chapter, we studied about Ishmael and his impact on the world. Next week we will study Isaac and his sons and grandsons. This week we will start a two-part "compare/contrast" paper. This does not need to be a real compare/contrast paper if you are not familiar with the format. It can simply be two pages, one for each man. The goal is to have a character sketch showing the differences between them. This week write about Ishmael. (There are some ideas for displaying your work after next week's research topic.)

● Continue to work on your report. This week, if you are finished with your information gathering, start organizing your notes, and start writing your rough draft.

Chapter 7

✱ In this chapter, we studied about Isaac and his sons and grandsons. Now it is time to write about Isaac. Display ideas: When you are finished with your paper, you could glue it inside a manilla file folder, along with a cover photo or illustration. Have fun, and make it look nice.

Deeper Research Topics for Older Students

● Continue to work on your report. This week, finish writing your rough draft, and work on editing.

Chapter 8

✳ Make a timeline of Joseph's life. Write the important happenings of each stage of his life. Look back at Chapter 7 for the beginning of his life. If you would like, you may illustrate your "Joseph's Lifetime" timeline.

● Continue to work on your report. This week, write you final draft and draw any pictures or maps you would like to include.

Chapter 9

✳ Try to locate a complete copy of Hammurabi's Code. Just for fun, make up your own Code of Conduct. Be careful, though, you will have to obey these laws, too!

● This is the last week for your big report project! Prepare and present your report to your family. Make sure you dress nicely, stand straight, speak clearly, and take the presentation seriously. If you can, ask friends and their families to come for your presentation, also. Ask your audience to take it seriously, too. Ask them for constructive criticism, and take notes on what you want to do better in your next presentation.

Chapter 10

✳ If you have an older sibling doing the senior high research assignments, or a sibling doing the junior high research assignments, team up for this assignment. Skim through Exodus, Leviticus, and Deuteronomy to find the details of what happened between the Exodus from Egypt and the entering of the Promised Land. Make a simple timeline project, showing the main points or events in the journey.

Deeper Research Topics for Older Students

Write the scripture references next to each entry. Also list the groups of people who already lived in Canaan.

● Work on the above assignment (with your sibling if you have one). This assignment will take this week and next to complete.

Chapter 11

✳ Continue working on the above assignment

● Work on the above assignment (with your sibling if you have one). When you are finished at the end of this week, decide how you are going to display what you have learned. Do a presentation for your family.

Chapter 12

✳ Research how silk was made in Ancient China. Write a one-page essay explaining the process.

● Research about the Mongols. Who were they? Who was their most famous leader? What major influences did the Mongols bring to Asia? Write a two-page paper explaining what you found.

Chapter 13

✳ Research the desert biome. What types of plants are indigenous to the Africa desert? What types of animals? Create a notebook page showing what you discover.

● Research to find out about the Sahara Desert. How big is it? Where exactly is it located? What kinds of people (if any) live there?

Deeper Research Topics for Older Students

Chapter 14

✱ In this chapter, we learned how the Israelites kept turning away from God. Why do you think humans do this? Do you think that God was "mean" to punish the Israelites? Write what you think and share it with your family.

● This week you will start your second large research project. Here is the assignment: Choose a main character in our story. (You may want to read ahead a chapter or two, or you may choose one that we have read about already.) This character may be one of the Children of Israel or from another nation. Write a paper detailing this character's life. You will need to research to gather more information on you character. You will be working on this assignment for the next five weeks.

Chapter 15

✱ After reading about the story of Samuel, write a four or five paragraph paper about his life.

● Work on your paper. This week, read at least two sources; one a day would be good way to plan. (Remember as you take notes, also write down the name of the resource and the author. You will need this information for your bibliography page.)

Chapter 16

✱ Research to find more about the culture of Crete. Draw pictures or write several paragraphs showing what you found.

● Continue to work on your report. This week, if you are finished with your information gathering, start organizing your notes, and start writing your rough draft.

Deeper Research Topics for Older Students

Chapter 17

✽ Research King Joash or King Josiah. Write a one page report about them.

● Continue to work on your report. This week, finish writing your rough draft, and work on editing.

Chapter 18

✽ Make a timeline of Daniel's life starting with his captivity. Write the important happenings of each stage of his life.. If you would like, you may illustrate your "Daniel's Lifetime" timeline.

● Continue to work on your report. This week, write you final draft and draw any pictures or maps you would like to include.

Chapter 19

✽ Research and write a page (or two) report about the Feast of Passover.

● This is the last week for your big report project! Prepare and present your report to your family. Make sure you include all of the improvements that you planned after your last presentation.

Chapter 20

✽ Do this project with an older sibling if possible and take two weeks to complete it. Using resources from Answers in Genesis™ and/or other creationists companies, find out everything you can about the Ica Stones. Write or create a project showing what you learned. (This may be a great opportunity to make a lapbook or display foldout.)

● Work on the above assignment with your sibling or by yourself.

Deeper Research Topics for Older Students

Chapter 21

✽ Work on the Ica Stone project which you started last week.

● Work on the above assignment with your sibling or by yourself.

Chapter 22

✽ Research the type of government the Romans adopted from the Greeks. What is a fasces? Why do we have this symbol in the United States of America?

● Research the influence of the Greek and Roman Empires on the rest of the world. Write at least two pages telling what you learned.

Chapter 23

✽ What is a Nazarene? What was the Nazarene vow? Research to find the answers to these questions. Also, find out who, in the Bible, took the Nazarene vow?

● Research Governor Herod. Who was he, and what kind of man was he? Write a character sketch about him.

Chapter 24

✽ Who is Gabriel the angel? Do some research on him and write a few paragraphs describing him.

● Augustus Caesar was an interesting character. He did not want people to call him "Emperor," yet that was exactly what he was. Why did the Roman Senate call him "First Citizen?" Write a few paragraphs about August Caesar.

Chapter 25

✽ Choose one of the disciples to write a character sketch about.

Deeper Research Topics for Older Students

● Do you believe that Jesus chose the disciples, with all of their varied backgrounds and characteristics, for specific reasons? Explain.

Chapter 26

✱ Why do you think Jesus waited until He was thirty years old to start His ministry?

● Research the Temple veil. Write a few paragraphs explaining the significance of the tearing of the veil during Christ's death.

Chapter 27 - 28

✱ &

● Research the early Church. Do a combined project explaining the growth and persecution of the Church following the death and resurrection of Christ.

Suggested Lesson Plan Outline

	Level 1 - early elementary	Level 2 - middle to upper elementary	Level 3 - Jr. High	Level 4 - Sr. High
Day 1	Listen to the first part of story, narrate orally & work on Journal pages	Listen to the first part of story, narrate orally & work on Journal pages	Listen to/read the story Work on Journal pages	Listen to/read the story Work on Journal pages
Day 2	Listen to the last part of story, narrate orally & work on Journal pages	Listen to the last part of story, narrate orally & work on Journal pages	Listen to/read the story Work on Journal pages	Listen to/read the story Work on Journal pages
Day 3	Complete timeline project and review chapter	Complete timeline project and review chapter	Complete timeline project and review chapter	Complete timeline project and review chapter
Day 4	Optional: hands-on projects	Optional: hands-on projects	Optional: Do hands-on project	Optional: Do hands-on project
Throughout week			Use Jr. High Level research packet to do deeper research topic Optional - Read assigned literature	Use Sr. High level research packet to do deeper research topic Optional - Read assigned literature

- Review 1 after Chapter 7.
- Review 2 after Chapter 14.
- Review 3 after Chapter 21.
- Final Review, followed by family show and tell night, after Chapter 28.

Review Activities Suggestions

- Make posters showing your favorite part of a chapter.
- Create a replica of a home or clothing article from the time period and civilization you are studying about.
- At the end of your review week, hold a show-and-tell for your family and friends.
- Cook a meal that goes with your time period and civilization.
- Listen to authentic ethnic music.
- Look at authentic ethnic art. (Be careful with this one - adult supervision required.)
- Use the optional hands - on projects included in the appendix of this book for your Review Week ideas. Have fun with it!
- Take picture of what you did and tape/paste them in your Student Journal. (Send them to me, too! I would love to see what you've done.)

Ancient Egypt Crafts

Building a pyramid out of sugar cubes is a super easy and fun project. You will need one box of sugar cubes for a pyramid with a 6 cube by 6 cube base. Use more cubes for a larger pyramid. To make a more permanent project you may glue it together using white craft glue or hold it together with straight pins.

Use a paper plate to make an Egyptian collar. This craft is best for small children.

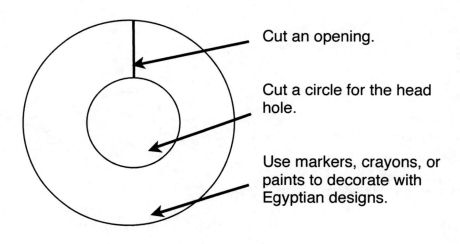

Cut an opening.

Cut a circle for the head hole.

Use markers, crayons, or paints to decorate with Egyptian designs.

Make an apple mummy.
  Supplies needed:
  - 1 Apple
  - 1 Popsicle stick
  - 1 Plastic bag (preferably a zip-lock freezer bag)
  - 1/4 cup of salt
  - 1/2 cup of sodium carbonate (powdered bleach)
  - 1/2 cup bicarbonate of soda (sodium bicarbonate, which is used as a raising agent in baking)

Here's how:

- Mix the salt, sodium carbonate, and bicarbonate of soda in the plastic bag.

- Create a face on your apple using the popsicle stick or butter knife.

- Next push the popsicle stick into the top of the apple to make a handle.

- Place the apple in the bag, making sure it is covered with the mixture

- Leave the bag open in a warm dry place and watch what happens.

Ancient Mesopotamian Crafts

I have always had a hard time finding craft projects for the Babylonian/Assyrian/Persian time period. Many of their practices were not something that I want my children emulating or turning into a "fun project." However, I have included two projects that would be fun and safe.

The first one is a 3D salt dough map of the Fertile Crescent. After you have formed your map, paint the great rivers and other features. This would be a fun and educational family project.

Here is a salt dough recipe.

You will need:

1 cup of fine salt
1 cup of flour
1/2 cup of water (may add more if needed)

Instructions:

1. In a large bowl or container, combine the flour and the salt.
2. Make a "well" in the flour/salt mixture and pour in the water.
3. Knead until the dough is smooth.
4. Shape it into a ball.
5. Wrap with plastic or store in air-tight container when not in use.

With this recipe, you add more flour to get a softer, more pliable dough. Adding more salt will give you a stiffer, more granulated dough. A softer dough will work best for this project.

After you are finished forming your map, let the dough dry for at least a week before you paint it. DO NOT use water color paints on your map. Oil paints or poster paints will work.

The second project also uses the above salt dough recipe. Make your own family "Code of Ethics and Behaviors" and "engrave" them on a stele made from salt dough. Again, let the dough structure dry before painting it.

(If your family completes one of the above projects, please take pictures and email them to me!)

Ancient Chinese Crafts

What is the first thing you think of when you think of China? Probably the Great Wall! Here is a fun way to construct your own Great Wall. You will need at least one whole set of Flora Craft Building Bricks ™. These handy, lightweight blocks stack just like bricks. Have fun and build a table top version of the Great Wall.

Learn to write in Chinese, but first make your own paper. You can find detailed instructions online, which tell you how to make your paper "from scratch," or there are paper making kits available at larger craft stores.

Make Chinese lanterns.

Make a Chinese meal and eat it in Chinese dining style.

Make and fly your own kite. Draw Chinese patterns and pictures on it!

Ancient Greek Crafts

Ancient Greek culture was so false - god - oriented, that it is difficult to find child-friendly projects.

However, we can thank the Greeks for the Olympic games, and this is something relatively safe to focus on for hands-on fun.

Idea:
Organize a family Olympics.
Decorate with the Olympic logo, and crown the winner with "loral leaf" crowns made from green construction paper.

Create your own Olympic torch.
You will need
- a small piece of white poster board
- tape
- orange, yellow, and red
  construction or wrapping tissue

paper
- markers/crayons/colored pencils

Here's how to do it: Roll the poster board into a cone shape to create the handle of your torch. Tape together. Cut out "flames" from your different colors of construction or tissue paper. Tape or glue them into the top of your torch. If you have aluminum foil, wrap it around the poster board handle. If you do not have the foil, color the handle silver or gold.

If you really want to get into it, bake a cake and decorate it with the Olympic rings.

Another fun project, reflective of the Greeks, is making mosaics. Craft stores have mosaic kits which allow you to create beautiful stepping stones for your garden or even coaster - sized mosaics.

Ancient Celtic Crafts

The Celtic people are known for their intricate handiwork and designs. Many of these designs have meanings in their origins.

Project idea:

You can make beautiful and intricate bookmarks with Celtic designs on them. Free printable Celtic bookmarks are easy to find online. Print and cut them out, and then color them with emerald green. Cover them with contact paper to make them last, and, if you desire, punch a small hole at one end for a tassel.

Project ideas:

Find some Celtic recipes to make a meal. Make place mats with the words "Céad Míle Fáilte," which means, "a hundred thousand welcomes." Use different shades of green paper with black lettering, and cover the place mats with contact paper to make them durable.

Make a potato meal! The Celts (who eventually settled in Ireland) liked potatoes.

Listen to some Celtic music. Our family loves the "Celtic Woman" group. They are from Ireland and have beautiful, lilting voices.

Ancient Indian Crafts

Ancient India was a land of intrigue! One of the most fascinating aspect of Indian art was ivory carving.

Go online or in a book to find an example of Indian ivory carving.

You could try your hand at "ivory" carving.
What you need:
Your parent (DO NOT use a knife without permission and supervision from your parent)
A bar of white soap (Ivory™ soap would work well!)
A knife

With a toothpick, sketch what you would like to carve into your soap
With your knife, carve away very small shavings of soap at a time.

Indian cuisine is delicious! Find some recipes and make an Indian family dinner.

Take it a little further and dress the part. Ladies in India wear saris (sorries). There are many places on line that can show you how to turn a few yards of fabric into a beautiful and authentic sari.

Ancient Roman Crafts

The Roman Empire was the biggest and strongest empire of the Ancient times. Roman soldiers dressed in armor and helmets when they went into battle.

In Ephesians 6, we are told to put on the Armor of God. When Paul wrote this, he was picturing the armor the Roman soldiers wore. This is a great time to make your own Armor of God. Use Ephesians 6 to help you. Write the name of each on the piece of armor. Cardboard and aluminum foil work great!

Use a cardboard box to make a diorama of a certain part of the story about the Roman Empires rise to power. For example, it could show the part of the story where Julius Caesar is kidnapped.

Make a salt dough map showing the Roman Empire.

Older children could place tiny flags in the exact location of important events during the rise of Roman power. Straight pins with tiny flags taped or glued to them would work well. Take it even further by color coding the flags. A certain color could signify an important battle, etc.

Optional Books and Movies

For elementary age children: because this time period is so full of myths and legends, it may be difficult to find age - appropriate literature.

- ☐ Tut's Mummy, Lost and Found
- ☐ The Greek News
- ☐ The Roman News
- ☐ George Muller (Missionary story)
- ☐ Missionary Stories with the Millers
- ☐ From Akebu to Zapotec

For upper-elementary through jr. high children: these are not exactly time-period exact, but they are good reads for this study.

- ☐ Twice Freed
- ☐ Treasures in the Snow
- ☐ The Tanglewood Secrets
- ☐ Star of Light
- ☐ The Bronze Bow

For jr. high and high school

- ☐ Theras and His Town
- ☐ The Golden Goblet
- ☐ Beyond the Desert Gate
- ☐ Archimedes

- ☐ Augustus Caesar's World
- ☐ The Cat of Bubastes
- ☐ Landmark book: The Pharaohs of Egypt

Movies the whole family would enjoy:

Ben Hur

Ten Commandments

The Prince of Egypt

Joseph - King of Dreams

Works Cited

Chapters 1-28

(1) Chapter 2
Answers in Genesis website:

http://www.answersingenesis.org/articles/2010/06/01/long-to-build-the-ark! "How Long Did It

Take for Noah to Build the Ark?"

written by Bodie Hodge (June 1, 2010) website visited on October 18, 2011(2) Chapter 6

Quote from, "The Patriarchs, Encountering the God of
Abraham, Isaac, and Jacob" written by Beth Moore, published by LifeWay Press,

©2005 ISBN 0-6330-9906-6

(3) All quotes from the Bible are from KJV, QuickVerse software, Electronic Edition STEP files, ©2005, Publisher location: Omaha, Nebraska

"Apologetics through Archaeology" section

section #2 http://www.answersingenesis.org/articles/am/v2/n4/geologic-evidences-part-one

Article by Andrew Snelling (September 18, 2007) website visited November 4, 2011 Section #3

http://www.answersingenesis.org/articles/am/v5/n2/dinosaurs-ark

Article by Buddy Davis (February 24, 2010) website visited November 4, 2011 section #13

"The Bible as History" [1] by Werner Keller, copy write 1981, page 145, first paragraph

Section #15
"The Bible as History" [2] by Werner Keller, copy write 1981, page 172, first paragraph

CPSIA information can be obtained
at www.ICGtesting.com
Printed in the USA
LVOW09s2201130317
527100LV00006B/372/P